PHILIPPIANS
AND
COLOSSIANS

MESSAGES OF PERSEVERANCE, RECONCILIATION, AND FELLOWSHIP

Light to My Path Series

Old Testament

Ezra, Nehemiah, and Esther
Isaiah
Ezekiel
Amos, Obadiah, and Jonah
Micah, Nahum, Habakkuk, and Zephaniah
Haggai, Zechariah and Malachi

New Testament

John
Acts
Romans
Philippians and Colossians
James and 1 & 2 Peter
The Epistles of John and Jude

Philippians and Colossians

Messages of Perseverance, Reconciliation, and Fellowship

F. Wayne Mac Leod

Authentic
MEDIA

Authentic Media
We welcome your comments and questions.
129 Mobilization Drive, Waynesboro, GA 30830 USA authenticusa@stl.org
and 9 Holdom Avenue, Bletchley, Milton Keynes, Bucks, MK1 1QR, UK
www.authenticbooks.com

If you would like a copy of our current catalog, contact us at:
1-8MORE-BOOKS
ordersusa@stl.org

Philippians and Colossians
ISBN: 1-932805-15-X

09 08 07 06 05   6 5 4 3 2 1

Published in 2005 by Authentic Media

Cover design: Paul Lewis
Interior design: Angela Duerksen
Editorial team: Bette Smyth, Carol Pitts, and Betsy Weinrich

Printed in the United States of America

Contents

Preface

I n his letter to the Philippians, the apostle Paul presented the Lord Jesus as an example of humility and meekness. He challenged the believers in Philippi to take the Lord Jesus as their example. Though he was in prison himself, the apostle encouraged the Philippians to live in the joy that comes from knowing the Lord Jesus. He reminded them that God was sovereign over all their trials and sufferings. Paul told them how the Lord was using his own suffering to accomplish great good for the church. In this letter Paul spoke to those who were suffering. He challenged them to lift up their heads and joyfully consider the Lord Jesus.

In his letter to the Colossians, Paul again presented Christ as the central theme. Paul spoke directly to the issue of legalism. He confronted the false teachers of the day and pointed the Colossians to the Lord Jesus and his work as being sufficient for their salvation. He demonstrated how Christ and his work alone is the means of salvation. He then challenged the believers of Colosse to live in freedom from the law. Paul concluded this letter with some advice about

● 1

personal relationships in the body of Christ. He encouraged each believer to press on to maturity.

I must confess that as I have been writing this commentary, I have not been in the best of health. There have been times when my thoughts have not been as clear as I would have liked. I trust, however, that the Lord God will bless this book and use it to encourage those who read it. Please read it with your Bible in hand. This is not a substitute for the Bible. Its purpose is to make the letters to the Philippians and Colossians clear and practical. I will consider this work a success if it brings you even a little closer to the Lord. May God use this book to inspire you in your relationship with him. Go out and share with others the truths you learn in this book. Let Paul speak again to you through this devotional commentary, and may the Spirit of God empower and encourage all who read it.

F. Wayne Mac Leod

Philippians

1

Thanking God for You

Read Philippians 1:1–11

Paul wrote this letter to believers in the region of Philippi. The city of Philippi was known particularly as a military settlement with many soldiers circulating in its streets. Here in this city, a wonderful work of God had begun through the ministry of Paul and Silas. We have the record of their visit to this region in Acts 16. Paul introduced a woman by the name of Lydia to the gospel. She opened her home to Paul, and a small church was established. It was not easy for Paul in Philippi. He was beaten and imprisoned in that city; but while in prison, he led a jailor and his family to the Lord. From this humble beginning, the Lord did a mighty work and established a powerful church in that area.

By the time Paul wrote this letter, the church had been well established. Notice in verse 1 that Paul and Timothy wrote to the saints in the region as well as to the overseers and deacons. This shows us that the work in Philippi had been growing in Paul's absence. Paul did not usually stay very long in any one place. He came long enough to preach the gospel and establish a leadership team but then left the new believers to continue what he had started.

Paul began this letter by reminding the church of the grace and peace that come from the Father and the Lord Jesus Christ. Grace is the unmerited favor of God. Peace has to do with being in harmony with God and his purposes in this world. There are many people in need of this unmerited favor and peace of God in their lives. Notice, however, that Paul spoke here to believers. Even believers need the favor and mercy of God. We all fall short of the standard God has for us. Grace is not only for the unbeliever. Followers of Christ are also in need of God's grace and his peace as well. As believers, our relationship with God is secure, but all too often we are not experiencing the peace that God intends us to have.

Paul's heart overflowed with gratitude to God for the Philippians. Every time they came to his mind, the apostle would thank God for them. Paul lived in this attitude of prayer. As he went through the day and the Lord brought people to his attention, Paul would lift them up to the Lord in prayer. We need to take a lesson from this. How often in the course of a day does the Lord bring people to our mind? Sometimes we may not have anything particular on our heart to pray for them, but we can thank God for them like Paul did.

Paul told the Philippians that every time he prayed for them, it was with great joy in his heart. The Philippians seemed to occupy a special place in Paul's heart. The church in Philippi had partnered with Paul in spreading the gospel. From the time that Paul met them, they had stood behind his ministry and persevered with him in prayer. Churches like this enabled Paul to continue preaching the gospel. Though they were not on the front line like Paul, they were still very important in the work of the kingdom.

Paul reminded the believers in Philippi that he was confident that the Lord who had begun a good work in them would complete that work (verse 6). Notice a couple of things in this verse. First, it is God who does the work. It is true that Paul had gone to the region of Philippi. He had preached the gospel there, and under his ministry people had come to Christ. But Paul did not see this as his own work. There was no doubt in his mind that the work of salvation in Philippi was the work of God. We need to understand this in our own ministries as well. We can try to do all we can to change those we love, but until the Lord intervenes and makes those changes possible, all our efforts will be in vain. Changing people's hearts is God's work. We are called to be instruments in the process of change, but it must be God who begins the work and brings it to completion.

How often have I tried in my own strength to change things in my life? I have often tried to pray more and discipline myself more. I have tried not to say certain things or think certain things. The reality of the matter, however, is that unless the Lord is in our efforts, there is no real hope of lasting change in our lives. While we must be willing partners, the strength and power must be his. When the Lord Jesus returned to heaven, he sent the Holy Spirit to live in the hearts of those who accepted him. True change must be the work of God through his Holy Spirit. We must stop trying to change things ourselves and let the Lord make those changes for us. God completes the work he began in us.

Second, notice in verse 6 that it is God's intention to continue working on us until his Son returns. Maybe you have met people who believe they have arrived at complete spiritual maturity. I have met individuals who have told me that they really had nothing more to learn about the Bible. This passage challenges this type of person. Paul tells us that God will not stop working on us until his Son returns. In other words, we may think we have arrived, but God knows better. He will continue to shape us and train us, showing us things we did not even know about ourselves that keep us from a deeper fellowship with him.

God will not give up. He is interested in completing what he has begun in our hearts and lives. Over the years God has shown me so many things that needed to be dealt with in my life. I have often cried out to him about these matters. My heart does long to be more like Jesus. Sometimes I wonder if I will ever be able to have victory. God promises me here that he will keep working on me. As long as God is working on me, there is hope. He is shaping me through all the circumstances of life. Some of those circumstances have been very difficult. Sometimes we resist his discipline and training. The challenge here, however, is for us to let him continue the work he has already begun in us. Paul was confident that God was going to continue his work with the Philippians.

Paul was in chains at this point in his life. Despite this, Paul had much to be thankful for. He rejoiced in prayer for the Philippians. His circumstances did not change his feelings toward them. He saw them as people who shared with him the special favor and mercy of God. They were co-workers with him and together they shared in God's great grace and mercy. God knew how much Paul longed for them in Christian love.

Paul prayed in verse 9 that these believers would experience more and more of the love of God and grow in knowledge and insight regarding his Word. Notice the balance here. Paul wanted them to experience the love of God in a deeper way, but this was closely connected to their knowledge of Scripture. Our love and experience of Christ and our knowledge of him as revealed in his Word must be linked. Some people emphasize loving God and downplay the importance of studying the Bible. Some emphasize knowledge of who God is but fail to truly love him with all their heart. Paul wanted the Philippians to grow in their love for God but also in their knowledge of him and his purposes. Only when the Philippians had found this balance could they truly be pure and blameless before God (see verse 10).

This balance of knowledge and love is the soil in which the fruit of righteousness grows (see verse 11). Churches and believers all around the world need to seek this balance. One church emphasizes love without knowledge; another emphasizes knowledge without love. This imbalance hinders spiritual growth. We must minister in love, but we must do so in the knowledge of truth. The fruit of true righteousness can only grow in a soil where love and truth are in balance. Only then can we bring true honor and glory to the Lord as churches and as individuals.

Paul reminds us that believers are not yet perfect. God has promised to continue the work he began in us. He wants us to grow not only in knowledge of him through his Word, but also in our experience of him in love. We must willingly surrender to our loving Father as he shapes and forms us into his image. Paul's heart cry for the believers of Philippi was that they allow God to continue the work he began in their lives.

For Consideration:

- What does this passage teach us about the heart of Paul for those he ministered to?

- What is in your heart for those you minister to?

- Why is it important for us to realize that the work of the kingdom is God's work, not ours? How does this change how we minister?

- What encouragement do you take from the fact that God desires to continue working with us until his Son returns? What are the areas in your life in which God needs to work?

- What do we learn here about the balance between truth (knowledge) and love? Have you found this balance in your church and personal life?

For Prayer:

- Ask the Lord to give you a greater passion for those you minister to.

- Thank the Lord that he is not yet finished with you. Ask him to deal with the issues that yet need to be dealt with in your life.

- Ask the Lord to give you a balance of truth and love in your church and personal life.

- Ask the Lord to forgive you for the times you have not surrendered to him and his work in your life.

2

Good from Evil

Read Philippians 1:12–19

One of the few certainties of life is that bad things will eventually come our way. It is often difficult to understand how these unpleasant things could ever produce anything good. Even the apostle Paul experienced difficult situations. At the time Paul wrote this letter, he was in prison for preaching the gospel.

In verse 12 Paul began by reminding the Philippians that what had happened to him had served to advance the kingdom of God. Paul had a dynamic ministry. Many people had come to know the Lord through his ministry. How could the imprisonment of the great apostle possibly advance the kingdom of God?

God's ways are very different from ours. What first appears to be a terrible thing can in fact result in our deliverance. As Jonah looked at the open mouth of the fish that came to swallow him, he very likely did not see it as his deliverance; but that is what it was. God could have used a more pleasant means of transportation to the beach that day, but he didn't. We do not always understand why God chooses to use the means he does, but we can be sure that he has a very good purpose.

In Paul's case the whole palace guard came to understand that Paul was in prison for the cause of Christ. This was no doubt a powerful testimony for the kingdom. Here was a man who was not afraid to stand up for his faith. Here was a man who was willing to commit his life to a cause he believed in.

On a trip to the Philippines, I heard the story of a missionary couple held hostage by an extremist group for a period of about a year. In the end, the man was killed. As I spoke with a missionary who had known this couple, he told me that the murdered man's testimony had stirred others to question whether they too were willing to die for the gospel. As a result many missionaries committed themselves more fully to the cause of Christ. All too often, we can become indifferent and lazy in our faith. Persecution can stir the body of Christ to action. In persecution the body of believers is strengthened. Hypocrites turn away, but those who are genuine become more committed to the cause. This is what was happening for Paul.

Paul reminded the Philippians that because of his chains others were being encouraged to be bolder (verse 14). They followed the example of Paul and became more courageous in sharing the message of the gospel. But Paul realized that not everyone was preaching with right motives; some were preaching out of envy. They were motivated by selfish ambition and were trying to promote themselves since Paul was in prison. However, there were those who were preaching out of sincere motives as well. These individuals understood that the apostle had been put in prison for the gospel and they took up the task of filling the void that had been created by Paul's absence.

There are things we will never understand about God and his ways. The great apostle Paul with all his potential was confined in a prison cell, while those who were preaching Christ out of selfish ambition were free. God's ways are perfect, however, and he had a purpose and a plan in all he was doing. Maybe you have been struggling in a small work for years, seeing little or no results. Maybe you have been confined to a bed in sickness. Maybe one problem after another seems to plague you. How easy it is to think that, because we face these circumstances, God must be punishing us. This, however, was not the case for the apostle Paul. God had a specific purpose in Paul's confinement. The Lord has a purpose for your trial as well.

Paul did not overly concern himself with what others were thinking and saying about him. He did not even really concern himself at this time about the improper motives behind the preaching of certain individuals. What was important for him was that the gospel was preached. Let's take a moment to examine this in more detail.

Paul is not telling us that it is acceptable to preach Christ with an intention to promote ourselves. We should all strive to preach Christ from pure motives. What Paul is telling us is that the Lord God can use anyone he chooses. We see evidence of this even in our day. Maybe you have heard preachers who have preached with the motive of having people think highly of them. These preachers work to gather a following for themselves. Maybe their motives are wrong, but God is still using them to reach souls with the gospel. These ill-intentioned individuals will certainly be judged one day and their motives exposed. Those who desire to be right with God will be careful to guard their motives and intentions. How we need to thank the Lord that he can use us with all of our imperfections! If he needed perfect people, none of us would be used.

There is a second point we need to make here. It is not our business to judge the motives and intentions of others. Paul left this matter to the Lord God. How quickly we often judge people's motives! Paul challenges us here to get on with the task of spreading the gospel. All too many people spend their time criticizing others. The church is filled with divisions and criticism. We divide over all kinds of issues. We don't like the way the church down the street worships or don't agree with their ministry focus, so we separate and condemn them. We fail to see how the Lord has chosen to use them.

It was true that Paul would have preached a different way, with different motives and intentions, but despite these differences the kingdom of God was moving ahead. Can you rejoice in the fact that the kingdom of God is advancing in the church down the street, even though they are different from your church? Can you rejoice in the fact that the preacher in the next town is seeing wonderful fruit in his ministry, even though he differs from you in some minor doctrinal issues? Paul's heart was to see people come to Christ and escape the flames of hell. He simply rejoiced that Christ was preached.

In verse 19 Paul reaffirmed his confidence in the Lord's purposes for his life. Paul was confident that as these believers joined him in prayer, the Holy Spirit would do a wonderful work through his suffering and trial. Paul would eventually be freed from his temporary distress, either in this world or the next.

I don't know what your particular struggle is today, but the same principle applies. God is in the process of maturing us and bringing us into a fuller knowledge of his Son. He is setting us free from the strongholds of sin in our lives. Sometimes the means he uses are quite strange to us, but he will still accomplish his purposes—of this we can be sure.

For Consideration:

- Have you ever seen God take something bad and use it for good in your life? Explain.

- What do we learn here about the purposes and plans of God? Does he always do things in the way we expect?

- What do we learn here about judging our brothers and sisters in Christ? What kind of relationship do you have with believers of other churches? Can you praise the Lord for the way he is using them?

- What is Paul's attitude in his trial? Do you have the same attitude?

For Prayer:

- Ask the Lord to forgive you for the times you have been guilty of judging your brothers and sisters in Christ because they were different from you.

- Thank the Lord that he can use all situations to accomplish his glory in our lives.

- Ask the Lord to give you the attitude of Paul in your trial. Ask him to give you a greater confidence in his purpose.

3

In Life or Death

Read Philippians 1:20–30

In the last meditation, we saw how Paul reminded the Philippians that the Lord God was able to use for good purposes the evil that had come into his life. Although Paul's time in prison was meant to hinder his ministry, God used it instead to spread the gospel. No matter what happens, our God is in control. We can take great comfort in this fact.

In this life we never really know what may come our way. God will call some to a path of trial and difficulty. The road they walk will be filled with obstacles. They will have opportunity to demonstrate the grace and power of God in overcoming difficulties. Others will live a life of relative ease and comfort. This too God will use to accomplish his glory in their lives for his kingdom. We dare not judge others based on the circumstances they face in life. God will put good people through the fire to refine them even more in preparation for what he has in store. It is important for us to honor God whether this is through trial or through ease.

Paul's great prayer for his life was that he would not be ashamed as he stood before the Lord Jesus. He wanted the Lord to be exalted in his life and in everything he did. Notice in verse 20 that he eagerly expected this to be the case. Paul could expect this because he gave everything to make this happen. He did his best to live a life that would bring honor and glory to the Lord Jesus. He reached out and used his gifts to bring glory and honor to his Savior. If God called him to remain on this earth, he would do so by bringing honor to Christ in the way he lived.

What a difference it would make in our lives if we shared Paul's life goal! Notice that Paul tells us that he wanted to honor the Lord Jesus whether that was "by life or by death." What circumstances are you facing right now? Do you see what Paul is telling us here? He is telling us that whatever God has for us, we are to make it our goal to honor him in those circumstances. This will not always be easy. Some will be called to sickness and suffering. God calls them to honor him in this sickness and suffering by their attitudes. Some will be persecuted. Again, they are to make it their greatest desire to honor the Lord Jesus in this. I remember an elderly gentleman I once met in Ontario, Canada. As we talked he told me that his greatest fear in life was that he would in some way dishonor his Lord—what an incredible life goal. I want my life to honor the Lord Jesus in the way I live. I want to honor him in my suffering and in my sickness. I want to honor him in my prosperity and my blessing. If I am persecuted and must face death for my faith, I want to do so honoring the Lord by how I die. This was the goal of Paul's life. It also should be our goal.

As Paul thought about the difficulties that face the believer, he reminded his readers that even if they were to make the ultimate sacrifice and lay down their lives for the

Lord Jesus, their death would be a gain for them because death would mean entering the presence of the Lord Jesus. For believers this will be the greatest joy. Notice, however, what Paul told his readers in verse 21. He told them that to live is Christ. We must not miss what the apostle is telling us here. He is telling us that while death is a blessing to the believer, so is life. If you know the Lord Jesus as your Savior, then to live is to experience his presence in your everyday life.

Some time ago I was lamenting the fact that I was facing much opposition in ministry. There seemed to be so many problems in the church I was working in. I brought this to the Lord. I prayed, reminding the Lord of the time in the Gospels when the disciples were with him on the Mount of Transfiguration. I told the Lord that I wanted to experience his presence as they did on the mountaintop that day. The Lord immediately reminded me of Daniel's three friends in the furnace. I saw the comparison the Lord was making: three friends on the mountaintop and three friends in the fiery furnace. Then the Lord spoke to my heart and said, "Wayne, do you really think that the three disciples on the mountaintop had a greater experience of God than the three in the furnace?" I thought about this for a moment and realized that the presence of God was equally as powerful in the furnace as it was on the mountaintop. What I am trying to say is this: God promises to be with us in life or in death. God is not only with us in the good times, he is also with us in the bad times. His presence is as real in one as in the other. Often we are blinded to his presence because of our trials. Paul reminds us that to die is gain, but to live is also to gain Christ and all that he offers.

One of the advantages of remaining here below for Paul was that he could continue to serve the church. To continue here on this earth would mean that he could be a greater blessing to others. Paul had a servant's heart; he did not live for himself. The desire of his heart in living was not to experience more of the pleasures of this life. It was not to accumulate more wealth and possessions. If Paul were to live, he would live with one goal in mind: to serve the Lord and to minister to his people. What is your goal?

Paul knew that believers needed him to remain on earth (verse 24). Paul did not fear death; he was ready to stand before the Lord. He had lived a full life that he was not ashamed of. However, he knew that his work was not yet completed. He needed to remain on this earth in order to finish the work that God had for him. With this in mind, Paul committed himself to remain and minister in Christ's name. Notice his goal in ministry in verses 25 and 26: he wanted to see the Philippians grow in the joy of their faith.

For a good part of my life, I pushed joy aside. I did not see the connection between joy and faith. For me, faith consisted of obeying the Lord and believing the right doctrines. I wrestled with the idea of a very personal and intimate relationship with the Lord Jesus that brought joy to my heart. I felt that as long as I was living in obedience and believing the right things, I was honoring God. It is very important for us to see that in this context of speaking about honoring God, Paul shows us the importance of joy.

The reality of the matter is that it is hard to honor the Lord God without joy. If you give an offering with a resentful heart, you do not honor the Lord. God loves a cheerful giver (2 Corinthians 9:7). If your heart is filled with anger and bitterness, you do not honor the Lord in your service for him. It is the desire of the Lord Jesus that we serve him with joy in our hearts. Psalm 100:2 says: "Worship the Lord with gladness; come before him with joyful songs." There is a wonderful passage in Psalm 85:6 that expresses what I believe revival is all about: "Will you not revive us again, that your people may rejoice in you?" The psalmist understood that revival happens when God's people find joy in him again. How often have we fallen into the heartless and joyless practice of faith? We do the right things and we believe the right things, but we have lost our joy. We need to be revived so that we find that joy again. Revived people have again found delight in God. They worship and serve with renewed, great joy in their hearts. This is what God desires. God is not interested in joyless faith. The faith that honors God is a faith that delights and rejoices in him. God wants us to be excited about him and what he has done. He wants us to find great joy in him. This was what the apostle Paul wanted to see in the lives of the believers in Philippi.

Paul challenged the believers in verse 27 to conduct themselves in a way that was worthy of the gospel. This would not always be easy. Notice that he told the Philippians that they would have to contend for the faith. The word *contend* means "to fight or wrestle." There are times when we will have to contend with the enemy, who wants to corrupt the faith by watering it down. We are not guaranteed a life of ease. Like Daniel's friends in the furnace, we will have to find our joy sometimes in the heat of trials and oppression, as we contend for our faith.

Paul was aware that there would be those who opposed the Philippians. He told them in verse 28 not to be afraid of these individuals. In times of strong opposition, these believers were to remind themselves that to die was gain and to live was to experience Christ and know his presence and enabling. Paul also reminded the Philippians that their godly and joyful lives would be a sign of destruction for those who opposed them. In other words, the failure of the believers' enemies to terrify them and halt the spread of the gospel of truth would be evidence of the church's ultimate victory and God's coming judgment on those who opposed it.

In Acts 5 the apostles were arrested and brought before the Sanhedrin to be judged. This Jewish ruling council opposed the teaching of the apostles and wanted to put them to death. Gamaliel, a respected Pharisee and teacher, cautioned them against such actions. Gamaliel warned the Sanhedrin: "I advise you: Leave these men alone! Let them go! For if their purpose or activity is of human origin, it will fail. But if it is from God, you will not be able to stop these men; you will only find yourselves fighting against God" (Acts 5:38–39). Those who opposed the Philippians found themselves in a similar situation. Opponents of the gospel could not stop the Philippians from believing, just as they could not stop the apostles. By opposing the believers, these enemies were fighting against God. This was a battle they could never win.

In verse 29 Paul told the believers that they had the privilege of not only believing in Christ but also suffering for him. To Paul, suffering for Christ was an honor. I have had opportunity from time to time to speak to those who fought in one of the great world wars. They would point to the scars they still bore on their bodies from bullets or other wounds inflicted on them, and they would speak with pride. For them it was an honor to bear the marks of suffering for their country. They did not complain. They understood that to fight for one's country involved suffering, and to bear the scars of battle was an honor. This was how Paul saw his suffering. He bore scars on his body where stones had struck him as he was being persecuted for preaching the gospel. There were whip marks on his back that spoke of his dedication to the cause of the Lord Jesus. This was nothing to be ashamed of. He was proud to have had the privilege of suffering for the cause of the Lord Jesus. How we need to have this attitude in our own lives today!

For Consideration:

• What is the goal of your life? What was Paul's goal? What stands in the way of you having Paul's goal for your life as well?

- What does Paul teach us here about the privilege of suffering for Christ? What things have you suffered for the cause of the Lord Jesus?

- What does Paul teach us about the reality of the presence of Christ in this life? Is it possible for us to focus so much on heaven that we forget that God calls us to live in his presence now?

- What role does joy have in our relationship with God?

For Prayer:

- Ask the Lord to fill your heart with joy as you serve him.

- Thank the Lord for the example of Paul in honoring the Lord in life or in death.

- Ask the Lord to give you more of this attitude.

- Ask the Lord to show you any way in which your life does not at present bring honor to him.

4

This Same Attitude

Read Philippians 2:1–11

The life of the apostle Paul was dedicated to the cause of Christ. In life or in death, he wanted to bring honor to his Lord. There were times when that desire brought him through some rough and difficult situations. He suffered tremendously for the cause of the Lord Jesus. In this next section the apostle Paul challenged the Philippians to adopt the same attitude as Jesus when they faced these difficult moments in life.

The apostle began by pointing the Philippians to the encouragement they had received from being connected with Christ. Paul reminded them that they could know the presence of Christ in life and death. In struggles as well as in blessings, the Lord was always there. The Lord Jesus would minister and comfort them in all their circumstances. The Philippians had experienced this comfort. When Paul used the word *if* in this verse, he was not questioning whether the

Philippians had ever been encouraged by being united with Christ. He knew that this was a reality for them already.

Notice in verse 1 that their encouragement came from being united with Christ. They were united with him in many ways. They were united with him in his death; that is to say, when the Lord Jesus died, he died for them personally. The Lord Jesus took their penalty on himself. They were also united with him in life. He had put his Holy Spirit in them and they belonged to him. The Lord's power flowed through them. The Holy Spirit united them with Christ and his desire and goal for their lives. What a blessing this was! They were joined together with the Lord of Lords and his purposes. They were his. They knew his presence. They shared his heart and his desire. They were one with the Lord in purpose, desire, and heart.

Being united with Christ was an encouragement for the Philippians. To encourage means to give courage. What courage it brings to God's people to know that they are united with Christ! When we are united with him, we can live with great boldness. We are not alone. We have victory because of Christ in us. We are strengthened by him and his power in us. What can the enemy do to believers after they have been united with the Lord Jesus?

Notice the second statement in verse 1: "if you have any comfort from his love." While none of these Philippians had personally met the Lord Jesus, they had certainly experienced his love. They had experienced the love of the Lord Jesus in what he had done for them. He had forgiven them of their sins. He lived in their spiritual hearts and spoke into their spiritual ears. In their struggles his presence was very real. They could not see him, but they knew him to be present. They could not hear his physical voice, but they knew what he was whispering into their ears. They felt his presence and knew his promises. They knew he loved them. What a comfort this was!

For a long time, I knew the doctrine of the love of the Lord Jesus for his people, but I was not open to the experience of that love in my life. I felt unworthy, and though I could not block the reality of his love, I certainly blocked my experience of it. I was not being comforted by his love because I was not letting him comfort me. This did not change the fact that he loved me, but it changed how I experienced his love every day. Paul assumed that the Philippians were open to experiencing the love of the Lord and being comforted by that love. They could come to Christ in their trials and allow him to comfort them. They could open their hearts to receive what he so longed to pour into them.

There is encouragement in being united with the Lord Jesus, and there is great comfort in his love. Notice in verse 1 that there is also "fellowship with the Spirit." The believer can experience communion with the Holy Spirit. The Holy Spirit comes to minister and teach us the things of God. He comes to guide us in all things. As we move from day to day, he leads, guides, and consoles us. He is the real presence of God in our hearts. He knows our thoughts and speaks in our minds and souls. We can go to him in our trials for counsel and advice. We can hear from him in those times when we do not know where to turn. There is no fellowship as sweet as the fellowship between the believer and the Spirit of Christ.

Paul reminded the Philippians that if they had experienced these blessings in Christ and had benefited from his tenderness and compassion, then they were to demonstrate this in their relationships with each other. They were to love their brothers and sisters with the love that they had received from Christ. They were to be one in spirit, even as the Holy Spirit had become one with them. They were to have one heart and one purpose, because they were connected to the same Lord and his purposes for them.

Notice that the Philippians were to love with the love they had received from Christ. They took as their example of unity the unity they had experienced with the Holy Spirit.

Notice one more thing in verse 2. Paul told them that his joy would be more complete if they lived in this close relationship with each other. Joy is a fruit of the Spirit. What we need to understand is that the *experience* of joy can be greater or lesser, depending on the circumstances. Paul's joy would not be taken away from him. He could experience joy as the fruit of God's Spirit in him, even in the midst of trials and tribulations. However, the immediate experience of this joy could become fuller, depending on the circumstances. The state of the church in Philippi could give Paul a much deeper experience of the gift of joy in his life.

There is a close connection between my experience of the fruit of the Spirit and my relationships with the members of the body of Christ. When things are not right in my relationships, my experience of the fruit of the Spirit will diminish. It is difficult to experience the fullness of the joy and peace of Christ when I am in conflict with fellow believers. Paul's experience of joy became greater when he saw his brothers and sisters in Christ loving one another. Our lives in the body are intimately connected. I can enable others to experience the joy and peace of the Lord in a much deeper way by my relationships with them.

In verse 3 Paul challenged the Philippians to do nothing out of selfish ambition or conceit. Instead, they were to put aside rivalry and pride in order to help others with their concerns. How easy it is to fall into the trap of wanting to get ahead of others! How many selfish decisions have I made in life? How much do I put the interests of my wife ahead of my own? What am I willing to sacrifice for my friends and loved ones? How many decisions do I make each day with my desires as the central focus? Paul challenges us to open our eyes and our minds to the needs of others.

He challenges us to consider others first in our decisions and actions. He calls us to die to ourselves and our own ideas and seek the best interests of those around us. Paul challenged the Philippians in verse 4 to look not only to their own interests but also to the interests of those around them. What a different world this would be if all believers were more interested in promoting others than themselves. How many problems in the church have resulted from those who arrogantly pushed other believers out of the way in order to achieve some selfish goal?

In verse 5 Paul told the Philippians that the Lord Jesus left us with an example of this unselfish lifestyle. In verse 6 Paul reminded them of how Jesus eternally has been God ("being in very nature God"), yet he did not consider the external display of his glory ("equality with God") something to be so prized or clung to ("something to be grasped") that he couldn't give it up for a season. In other words, though Jesus was God, he loosened his grasp on some of the privileges pertaining to the divine nature. For a season he chose to live as a simple man. The men and women he met on this earth did not honor him as they did the Father. Though he was equal to the Father, he did not claim special rights, but allowed men to spit on him and curse him. Though he deserved all honor and praise, he denied himself these privileges as he walked on this earth.

Jesus took on the nature of a servant (verse 7). He became truly human like us (but without sin). In his human body, he was subservient to the law and to his parents. He allowed himself to suffer all that we suffer. He was tempted just as we are. He felt the hurts and pains that we feel. As a simple, humble man, Jesus also demonstrated his true servant nature by his complete obedience to the Father (verse 8). Jesus depended entirely on the Father for his life and willingly suffered death for his very own creation. The Lord Jesus even submitted to the humiliation of dying as a criminal on a cross, for the whole world to see.

Why did he do this? He did it for you and me. He did it so that we could have a relationship with God. The Lord Jesus died, taking our penalty, so that we could go free. He did not consider himself. He put aside some of his divine privileges for a time. He put aside the honor that was due him. He suffered the shame of death on a cross. God is a spirit and cannot die a physical death, but Jesus took on a physical, human body and died a physical death. In all this, he was not thinking of his personal comforts and preferences. He was only thinking about us and our salvation. This, says Paul, is how we need to live our lives—just like Jesus. We are to put aside our pride. We are to lay ourselves down for the cause of our brothers and sisters. Our lives are to be given over to serving others, just as Jesus served us.

Notice in verse 9 that Christ's actions did not go unnoticed by God the Father. The Lord Jesus was exalted to the highest position because of his obedience. God gave him a name that would be honored by all nations and tribes. His name was lifted higher than all other names. Every knee will one day bow to the Lord Jesus. All creatures in heaven and earth and under the earth (those who have died as well as any demonic being) will recognize him as Lord and bow before him in reverence and respect. They will honor the Son to the glory of the Father. There is no competition here between the Father and the Son. To honor one is to honor the other. To worship the Son is to worship the Father. Jesus is God and equal to the Father in nature and equally deserving of praise and honor.

Christ's victory came through humbling himself. This is the challenge of Paul to the Philippians. He challenged them to take the Lord Jesus as their example. Maybe you are a pastor or spiritual leader in your church. Are you willing to put aside the dignity of that position and die to your own interests and rights, as Jesus did, to minister to the needs of those around you? Jesus laid aside his rights for the purpose of reaching this world. He calls us to do the same. He seeks a people who will risk all and die to all their own ideas and dreams for the sake of the kingdom. He calls us to take on the attitude of the Lord Jesus as we move forward to expand the kingdom of Christ. What we have received from him we are to share with others. He is our example.

For Consideration:

- Paul speaks here about encouragement in unity with Christ, comfort in his love, and fellowship with his Spirit. Have you experienced these truths in your life? Give examples.

- What things have you accomplished in life that you are proud of? How does this affect your relationship with those around you? Would you willingly put all this aside to minister to a brother or sister in Christ?

- How do your relationships with other believers affect their experiences of the fruit of the Spirit?

- How many decisions in life do you make based on your own interests and desires? What is the challenge of this passage?

For Prayer:

- Ask the Lord to help you to live your life with a greater focus on the needs of others.

- Thank the Lord for the encouragement of unity with him, the comfort of his love, and the fellowship you have with his Holy Spirit.

- Ask the Lord to forgive you for the many times you have been too selfish to consider the needs of others around you.

- Thank the Lord Jesus for how he lived his life with you in mind. Thank him for his continued interest in your needs.

5

No Grumbling

Read Philippians 2:12–18

I n the last meditation, we saw how Paul challenged the
Philippians to have the attitude of the Lord Jesus in all
they did. He encouraged them to consider the interests of
others as being more important than their own. He pointed
them to the example of the Lord Jesus and challenged them
to follow his example in their relationships with each other.

When Paul had been with the Philippians, they had
listened to his advice and obeyed the Lord. Now in his
absence, he was confident that they would be even more
diligent (verse 12). He encouraged them not only to follow
the example of the Lord Jesus in their relationships with
each other but also to work out their salvation with fear and
trembling.

What does it mean to work out our salvation? Paul made
an interesting statement in verse 13. He told the Philippians:
"It is God who works in you." The Philippians needed to do
the *working out* but God would do the *working in*. The term

work out is often used today to speak of physical exercise. When we talk about working out, we mean we are following an exercise routine. Paul seems to be telling the Philippians that they were to work out or routinely exercise what God was working in them.

God gives us everything we need to live and serve him. He gives us his Holy Spirit to work in us and through us. While God works his salvation into us, it remains our responsibility to exercise that salvation by living in obedience to the ministry of the Holy Spirit. To work out our salvation is to exercise our faith by living in obedience to God. It is to flex our spiritual muscles and strengthen the gifts that God has put in us.

Notice in verse 12 that we are to exercise the salvation that God has given us with "fear and trembling." We are to do this because God is working this salvation in us according to his good purposes. In other words, God is shaping us according to his purpose. The Holy Spirit himself is working in us and leading us in the purpose and plan of God. This is something we dare not take lightly. The Spirit of God is doing a powerful and awesome work in us. How little we appreciate this reality! Listen carefully to what Paul is saying here: God is working in you. Your spiritual growth is not a result of your own efforts. It is the result of the powerful work of a holy and almighty God who has chosen to touch your life and do a mighty work in you. What is your response to this? Should we not take God's work in us very seriously? Would it not be a very fearful thing to fight against what the Spirit of God is doing in us? Those who truly understand this concept will exercise the gifts God has been working in them. They will choose to live in obedience to the leading of his Spirit. They will demonstrate to all the fruit the Spirit is producing in them. These individuals tremble at the reality of God in them. They fear not so much in the sense of being afraid but in terms of deep desire to honor and respect the work that God is doing in and through them. They do not take lightly what God is doing.

Paul reminded the Philippians that since God was working in them and through them, they had no reason to grumble about what he was doing. In his sovereignty, God brought them through circumstances as he saw fit, "according to his good purpose." The Philippians were to respect God and his purposes enough that they would willingly accept what God brought their way. They were to do everything without complaining and arguing (verse 14). To complain and argue is to disagree with what God is doing. There have been things I have gone through in life that did not seem pleasant at the time, but I have lived long enough to realize that God did have a purpose for these trials in my life. My quarrelling with God only showed that I did not trust what he was doing in me.

Paul reminded the Philippians in verse 15 that they were to resist murmuring and bickering so that they could be blameless and pure children of God. The desire of God is to produce children who are "without fault in a crooked and depraved generation." The Lord wants us to be examples and lights to a world that is lost in sin and rebellion. He wants to make us shine like stars in the dark sky of this world. In order to do this, God works his salvation into every corner of our lives. This means that he will have to discipline and train us. This will not always be easy. Some of us will pass through extremely difficult times, but all who submit to God during tribulation will come forth like stars shining in the darkness. Athletes must train and discipline themselves if they hope to be triumphant. The same is true for soldiers. In our spiritual lives there are times when we must face hardship. Sin and rebellion must be crushed and removed. Strongholds and bad habits must be defeated. All this can be painful, but it is for our good. We must let God move in us to accomplish his purposes, no matter what the cost. We must resist complaining and grumbling and open ourselves to let the Lord do his powerful work in us.

In verse 16 Paul challenged the Philippians to hold out the word of life so that he would be proud of them in the day Christ returns. His desire was that they would strongly offer the word of God to the lost souls around them. There would be plenty of temptations to neglect this duty. How many believers have failed to carry their light into a dark world? How many have turned their backs on the Lord Jesus in the midst of opposition? How many have watered down Scriptures to suit their needs and interests? Paul did not want to see the Philippians fall into this trap. He wanted them to hold tightly to these words as their guide into truth and righteousness and offer the word of life to a lost world.

Paul reminded the Philippians in verse 17 that he himself was being poured out like a drink offering because he was remaining true to the word of life in his service to God for the Philippians. In his ministry for their growth in the faith, he had to suffer. Paul was willing to do this and would rejoice, even if his life had to be poured out for them. He would be faithful, no matter the cost. He would willingly sacrifice all so that they would grow in Christ.

Paul was able to rejoice in his suffering. He was able to rejoice because he knew that God was working into him a greater measure of grace and maturity. Are you able to rejoice in your present suffering or trial? Remember what Paul is telling us here. God is working his salvation in us. He is working his purposes into our lives and hearts. His purposes are for our good. Instead of complaining about our lot, we need to have Paul's attitude and learn to rejoice because God is doing a good work in us.

For Consideration:

• What does Paul mean when he tells us that we are to work out our salvation?

- Why should we work out with fear and trembling the salvation that God is working into us? Have you caught a sense of what Paul is telling us in this passage?

- How often have you found yourself complaining because of your circumstances? What does Paul have to teach us about this matter?

For Prayer:

- Ask the Lord to give you a deeper sense of fear and trembling as you work out what he is working into your life.

- Thank the Lord that he is actually working his salvation into every corner of your life.

- Ask him to give you a heart that is open to him and what he is doing.

- Ask the Lord to forgive you and give you grace to accept the circumstances he is using in your life to bring you closer to him.

6

Timothy and Epaphroditus

Read Philippians 2:19–30

There is a very special relationship between believers. In the Lord Jesus, we are bound together in a wonderful bond that spans culture, language, and age. I remember a trip to the Philippines some time ago. I was asked to tell briefly about my distribution ministry. After I spoke, the pastor invited the audience to come forward to pray for me and this ministry. What a blessing it was for me to see these leaders gather around me and pray for the blessing of God on my writing and personal life! Prior to this time, we had never met; now we stood with hearts united, calling on God to bless and to minister. This was possible only because of the spiritual bond that exists among believers. We see evidences of this wonderful bond in the closing verses of Philippians 2.

Paul told the Philippians in verse 19 that it was his desire to send Timothy to them. Remember that Paul was in prison, so a visit from him was not possible. He decided instead to send Timothy to see how things were going in the church. Timothy would return to Paul with news of the church. Notice that Paul was confident that the news he would hear would be positive. He expected to be cheered by this news.

We need to see two things in this verse. First, notice the confidence Paul had in the believers of Philippi. His words were encouraging, though he was not beyond correcting when correction was necessary. In this case, however, he had great confidence in the fact that these believers would advance the cause of Christ during his absence because the Holy Spirit was leading and strengthening them. Paul was eager to hear news about the Lord's work in Philippi because he was confident in what the Spirit of God could do through the church there.

Second, notice Paul's love for the Philippians. Paul did not preach to them and leave them. He wanted to know what had been happening to them. How many wonderful preachers have come through your church? How many of them have actually shown enough interest in you to come back just to see how you were doing? The Philippians were not just a statistic on paper. They were real people that Paul loved so much that he had to send Timothy to see how they were doing.

Notice in verse 20 that when Paul sent Timothy, he did so knowing that there was no one like him. Timothy had a genuine concern for the Philippians. He shared the heart of Paul for the welfare of these believers. When Paul sent Timothy, he was sending the very best he could. Timothy had proven to all that he was selfless in his ministry (see verse 21). Timothy was not in the ministry to pursue his personal ambitions. There are many individuals in ministry for themselves. They serve the Lord so that others will look at them and honor them as great spiritual leaders. They enjoy the attention. This was not the case for Timothy. He was not looking out for his own interests but for those of the Lord

Jesus. He was a servant of the Lord and put aside his own fame, ease, and gain for the cause of Christ. Timothy had proven that he was willing to sacrifice everything for his Lord.

There was another way that Timothy had proven himself. "As a son with his father," Timothy had served with Paul in the work of the gospel (verse 22). There are several things we need to understand by this statement. First, we need to see Timothy's faithfulness. He had served with Paul in the struggles and the good times. He never gave up. He persevered through the obstacles on the pathway. He was not a quitter. Paul was not always an easy person to work with. He had a very strong passion in ministry. That passion drove him to places that most people would never have gone. Timothy had been there beside him all the way. When Paul was stoned, Timothy was there too. When Paul was driven from towns and cities for preaching the gospel, Timothy went with him, proving himself to be faithful and reliable.

Notice that Paul particularly mentioned that Timothy had served with him as a son. There is an element of humility here. Timothy was happy with the role of a son. He respected Paul and served under him. He did not seek his own interests but the interests of the Lord. He had proven that he could work as a son under Paul. He did not need to be in control. It is one thing to be a leader and another to be a faithful follower. Timothy was happy to remain in a helper role. We have met individuals in ministry who very quickly want to be in charge. They strive for the top position. Timothy served faithfully as a son, in the role of second place and did so with a contented heart. This says a great deal about Timothy. It was for this reason that Paul had every confidence that he could send Timothy.

There are many people who want to be in a position of responsibility who have never proven themselves in the small things. They want to be leaders, but they have not proven to be faithful as followers. They want to be in first place, but have never learned to be in second place.

In verse 24 Paul told the Philippians that he was confident that he would be set free to come to them as well. This was at least Paul's hope. His desire was to be set free. We need to understand, however, that though he did not delight in being held in a prison, he still rejoiced there in the Lord (see verse 17). It is not always easy to rejoice when we find ourselves in a situation we do not like. This, however, was exactly where Paul was. He would give anything to be able to leave his prison cell, but he would not let that prison cell take away his joy. Maybe you find yourself in this kind of situation. Maybe you are in a place you do not like. Maybe it is your work or the city you are living in. As you remain in this situation, you find that your joy is being stripped from you. We all need to learn the art of not letting circumstances rob us of the joy of the Lord.

In verse 25 we meet an individual by the name of Epaphroditus. In Philippians 4:18 we read that Epaphroditus had been sent to Paul with gifts for him in his need: "I have received full payment and even more; I am amply supplied, now that I have received from Epaphroditus the gifts you sent. They are a fragrant offering, an acceptable sacrifice, pleasing to God." Epaphroditus was sent by the church in Philippi as an expression of their concern for Paul in his need. Here in verse 25, however, Paul sent Epaphroditus back to them.

It is important to note that Epaphroditus was not being sent back because of any failure on his part. Paul made it clear in verse 25 that he was a brother, fellow worker, and fellow soldier. In saying this, Paul told the Philippians that Epaphroditus was dear to him not only as a brother but also as a very useful servant of the gospel.

The reason why Paul felt compelled to send back

Epaphroditus was that he was very distressed. He had been ill and the news of his illness had reached the church in Philippi. Epaphroditus, according to Paul, had almost died; however, God had saved his life. Paul reminded the Philippians that in sparing the life of Epaphroditus, God had also spared Paul from tremendous sorrow, for he loved this man dearly.

Epaphroditus knew how concerned the church in Philippi had been for him. For this reason, he wanted to go visit them so that they could see for themselves that he was well. Paul saw this desire in the heart of Epaphroditus and decided to send him back to comfort the church in Philippi. He challenged the church to welcome him back with great joy. He also encouraged them to honor men like him because it was for the gospel that he risked his life. He had become ill in the course of his service for Paul. For this reason, Paul commended him to the church.

We see something of the family relationship that existed in the church of that day. We see the devotion of the church of Philippi to Paul in his need by sending a gift through Epaphroditus. We see the willingness of Epaphroditus to risk his life for Paul. We also see the devotion of Timothy to minister alongside Paul and the tremendous confidence and respect that Paul had for Timothy in return. We also see how concerned Timothy was for the welfare of the church in Philippi. Paul too shared that deep concern for the church. The hearts of these believers overflowed with love and devotion to each other. What an example this is for us in the body of Christ in our day.

For Consideration:

• What do we see in this passage concerning the relationships among believers in the church of that day? How does your church compare to this?

- Paul told the Philippians that Timothy ministered in a selfless way. What does it mean to minister in a selfless way?

- Have you ever found yourself in a place you did not like? Did this rob you of your joy?

- What is the challenge of this passage to us today?

For Prayer:

- Ask the Lord to help you to rejoice in your circumstances.

- Ask the Lord to give you the faithfulness and humility of Timothy.

- Ask the Lord to renew love and devotion to one another in your church fellowship.

7

No Confidence in the Flesh

Read Philippians 3:1–9

Paul challenged the Philippians to rejoice in the Lord. This particular call to rejoice in the Lord comes in the context of a warning for them to watch out for those who were trying to get the Philippians to put confidence in the flesh (see verse 3). The church of Philippi was under attack. There were false teachers instructing believers to return to the laws of Moses if they wanted please God.

What is important for us to notice is that the rejoicing was to be "in the Lord" (verse 1). These believers were not called to rejoice in their own efforts. They were not called to take great delight in telling God all the good things they had done for him to merit salvation. Their rejoicing was to be in the Lord. The Lord had done everything necessary. He had broken the power of sin. He had died so that they could be forgiven. He had opened the door for them to enter the presence of God. He had sent his Holy Spirit to live in their hearts. All rejoicing was to be in what the Lord Jesus had done.

Notice how Paul told the Philippians in verse 1 that this rejoicing in the Lord Jesus along with what he had written to them provided protection against the doctrinal error that was spreading through the region. If we learn to rejoice in the Lord and his work, we will be protected from all kinds of spiritual errors. All Christians need to spend time thinking of what the Lord Jesus has done. We need to learn how to rejoice, delight, and trust in his work. This will protect us from the enemy, who tries to get our attention off the Lord Jesus and onto ourselves and what we have accomplished. This was the error into which the false teachers in Philippi had fallen.

Paul clearly stated what he believed about false teachers. He called them dogs in verse 2. Remember that the dog was an unclean animal in Bible times. This was how Paul saw these teachers: they were unclean animals. There was a second reason why Paul called them dogs. He did so because they were "mutilators of the flesh." Very likely, Paul was saying that they took great delight in the doctrine of circumcision. This ceremonial ritual seemed to be their focus. They believed that the only way a man could truly be a believer was if he submitted to being circumcised. Like hungry dogs, these false teachers were mutilators of the flesh. As a Jew, Paul had been circumcised. However, here Paul spoke of circumcision as a mutilation of the flesh. He did this because he no longer saw any spiritual significance in the practice. The false teachers in Philippi, however, taught that if people were not circumcised, they could not be saved.

In response to these objections, Paul told the Philippians that the person who was truly circumcised was the one who worshiped God by the Spirit and gloried in the Lord Jesus. In the Mosaic law, circumcision was a sign that an individual belonged to the nation of Israel. What sign is there in our day that shows that we belong to the family of God? That sign is the presence of the Holy Spirit in our lives. It is the Holy Spirit who has been given to us as a sign and seal that we are children of God (Ephesians 1:13–14; Romans 8:9). You can be baptized and belong to a church, but if you do not have the presence of the Spirit of Christ in your life, then you do not belong to him. Paul clearly tells us in Romans 8:9 that "if anyone does not have the Spirit of Christ, he does not belong to Christ." The sign of belonging to the Lord Jesus is that the Spirit of God lives in your heart.

Those who truly belong to the Lord Jesus today are those who are led by the Spirit of Christ to worship and glorify their Lord. These individuals put no confidence in the flesh. They know that they can go to church regularly and not be a child of God. They know that they can be baptized and still not be part of his kingdom. The only sign and proof that can be trusted is the presence of the Spirit of Christ in their lives. When the Lord looks on us, this is all he is looking for. He is looking to see if the Spirit of his Son dwells in us. When it comes to salvation nothing else matters. It is true that we will be judged for how we have worked out that salvation in our daily experience. Paul makes it clear in 1 Corinthians 3:14 that there were individuals whose works would be "burned up" but they themselves would be saved "as one escaping through the flames." In regard to salvation, however, those who belong to Christ have understood the importance of his work and have placed all their confidence in him and what he had done.

Paul reminded the Philippians that if there was anyone who could have put confidence in the flesh it was he. Paul had been circumcised on the eighth day, as every good Jew was. He belonged to the tribe of Benjamin and considered himself a Hebrew of Hebrews. By birth, he was a pure Jew. In practice also, Paul had lived out his Jewish faith. He had been a member of the Pharisee sect. The Pharisees were known for their strict adherence to the laws of Moses. No one in Israel was more careful than the Pharisees to precisely obey the Mosaic law. In regard to zeal, Paul had been more zealous than anyone of his time for the cause of the Jewish faith. He had persecuted the Christian church because he had once believed it to be a threat to his Jewish faith. He had believed that God had chosen him to rid the world of the threat of Christianity. He could not be surpassed when it came to religious human effort.

Paul reminded the Philippians that when it came to legalistic righteousness, he was faultless. When Paul spoke of legalistic righteousness, he meant ceremonial obedience to the law. If you were to examine Paul on the basis of externally keeping the laws of Moses, he was meticulous. Maybe you have met individuals like this. They seem blameless in their human efforts to please God. They go to church, read the Bible, pray every day, and do many good works. They are faithful in their relationship with God and cannot be faulted in the things they believe.

What is important for us to understand here is that while Paul was outwardly righteous, he was still lost in his sin. This is hard for people to understand. How can a man or woman who does the right things be lost in sin? Paul told the Philippians in verse 7 that he considered all the advantages of external status and performance to be completely worthless compared to what Christ offers. In saying this, Paul distinguished between the way of human righteousness and the way of Christ's righteousness. Paul came to the place in his life where he forsook what the law offered and turned to Christ and what he offered.

Verse 8 shows us that Paul had tried the way of ritualistic righteousness. He had carefully followed the law, but one day he found another way. The Lord Jesus appeared to him and changed his life. When Paul met the Lord Jesus, he found something the law could never give. In verse 9 Paul told the Philippians that in Christ he found true and complete righteousness. Righteousness has to do with being in a right relationship with God. This is something the law could never give. The law could never completely deal with sin in the hearts of men and women. The law offered a temporary covering for sin but did not erase the condemnation. It could not change the hearts of men and women. Christ, on the other hand, dealt with sin finally. His sacrifice completely and eternally satisfied all God's legal requirements. Never again would there have to be another sacrifice for sin. God places his Holy Spirit in the hearts of those who accept him. He leads and guides believers, enabling them to live the life they could never live in their own strength. Those who accept the work of Christ on their behalf enter a relationship with God that can never be taken from them. Paul then proclaimed that his desire was for the righteousness of Christ (verse 9). In the way of Christ, there is complete forgiveness and peace with God. In the way of Christ, there is power to accomplish what can never be accomplished by human effort.

What Paul is telling us here is that there is the way of legalistic righteousness and there is the way of Christ's righteousness. Legalistic righteousness is man-made. It comes as a result of discipline and self-denial. It promotes salvation by human effort. People who believe in this approach think that their good works can please God and earn them a place in his kingdom. By contrast, Christ's righteousness is a gift given to any unworthy sinner who asks. Those who accept this righteousness know that they are unworthy of it but open their hearts to receive by grace what they do not deserve.

The righteousness that comes from God is "by faith in Christ" rather than human effort (verse 9). We are not made right with God because we have done the right things. We are made right with God because God has chosen to forgive our sins and cast them from us. Those who open their hearts to the Lord Jesus and his work are forgiven for their sins. They are clothed with the Holy Spirit who comes to live in their hearts. The Holy Spirit gives them a new life and a new nature. While their old nature is sinful and not acceptable to God, this new nature is without sin. It is the life of Christ in them. That life is not yet completely formed in them, but it is growing. Believers are to open their eyes to this new nature and live in it.

There is something very liberating in this thought. I will be saved not on the basis of how good I have been but rather on the fact that Christ has put his life in me. There are unsaved people who live better lives than we do as believers. Sometimes these individuals will put us to shame in their zeal and knowledge of the Word. They may, like Paul, be legalistically righteous, but they still do not belong to the Lord Jesus. The Spirit of Jesus does not live in them. They have religion and doctrine, but they do not have the life of Christ.

What Paul discovered was Christ. He discovered that it was not important how good he was but whether he had the life of Christ in him. That life and righteousness is a gift given to those who will simply open their hearts to receive it. You don't have to be perfect, but you do need the Lord Jesus.

For Consideration:

- How does rejoicing in the Lord protect us from error?

- What is the one sign that guarantees that we belong to the Lord Jesus?

- What is the difference between legalistic righteousness and the righteousness that comes by faith?

- What is the difference between preaching Christ and preaching the law?

- How does what Paul teaches here influence how we live our lives? How does it change our understanding of God?

For Prayer:

- Ask the Lord to help you to rejoice more in him.

- Thank the Lord that you do not have to merit your salvation, because it is given to you as a free gift.

- Do you know people who are trusting in their legalistic righteousness? Take a moment to pray that God would open their eyes.

8

Pressing On

Read Philippians 3:10–16

I n the last meditation, we saw how Paul told the Philippians that his greatest desire in life was to know Christ and his righteousness. Paul had tried religion and good works, but that had left him empty and dry. When he found the Lord Jesus, he found what his heart had been longing for. Now his whole desire was to grow in Christ and in the knowledge of him. Paul continued on this theme.

Notice in verse 10 that Paul told the Philippians that he wanted to know Christ. The reality of the matter was that he already knew him. Paul's heart, however, was not content to know Christ in the way he presently knew him. Paul wanted to know Christ in an even greater way. This is where we all need to be. We all need to have hearts that cry out to know Christ more than we presently know him. All too many believers stop at their salvation. They come to know the Lord Jesus at their salvation but don't seem to grow much from that point. The great apostle Paul tells us that he wanted to know Christ more. How much more should we want to know him! How content we are to know so little of him! How foolish it is for us to believe that we truly know him at all! He is far bigger than our greatest ideas of him.

It is important that we see in verse 10 that Paul not only wanted to know Christ more, but he wanted to know the power of his resurrection. What is resurrection power? It is the power that conquered death. Jesus died on the cross, but death could not hold him. In resurrection power he rose from the dead. In resurrection power he went to be with his Father. This is the power that Paul wanted to know. Resurrection power is the power that conquers sin and death in this world. It is the power to overcome sin. It is the power to pass through death and into the presence of the Father, just as Jesus did. This is the greatest power that exists. It is wonderful to see the Lord heal an individual of an illness or infirmity. This is truly a demonstration of power. What is an even greater demonstration of power, however, is the power to overcome sin and death and to enter into the presence of God the Father. Paul wanted to live in this resurrection power. He wanted to conquer sin and death. He wanted to know Christ and to experience his power over this world of sin and evil. He wanted to know the power to rise victoriously in the end and to enter into the presence of Christ forever.

This victory over sin and death would not come easily. Paul had already experienced much suffering in his life. The enemy had lashed out at him. Satan had stirred many people to seek Paul's life. Paul told the Philippians, however, that he also wanted to know the fellowship of sharing in the sufferings of Christ. He was willing to face suffering and hardship. He wanted to know the fellowship of Christ in that suffering. He wanted to share with Christ in the trials of advancing the kingdom. He would not back down. He would not give up the battle. He would stand his ground and endure as his Savior had endured. He wanted to be like Christ in his death. He wanted to be faithful to the end. He wanted to live for Christ and was willing to die for Christ, knowing that one day he too, like Christ, would rise from the dead and enter the presence of his heavenly Father.

What Paul is telling us is that knowing Christ is not always easy. Sometimes the Lord will take us through great trials and difficulties. Who among us has not grown to know the Lord Jesus in a much deeper way through trials? If you want to know Christ, you will have to be willing to face the difficulties as well as the good times.

Paul reminded the Philippians in verse 12 that he had not yet arrived at a complete knowledge of Christ. Paul still needed to grow in his character. He was far from perfect in his relationship with God. Paul did not hesitate to tell the Philippians that he was not sinless. There are many leaders who would have us believe that they are fully mature. They are afraid to admit that they have not yet arrived at perfection because they feel that people will not respect them. Paul did not have this fear. He openly admitted that he had a long way to go in his relationship with Christ.

If you are a spiritual leader, you need to realize that those under you already know that you are not perfect. They have seen you fail. Instead of spending time trying to maintain a false image, you need to do what Paul did. He pressed on to take hold of the goal that Christ had for him. The phrase *pressed on* indicates that this effort would not be without difficulty. Paul would have to face many trials in this pursuit of the goal that Christ had for him. Notice, however, that Paul knew that the Lord Jesus had a purpose in mind when he chose him. The Lord Jesus had rescued him from sin for a reason. Paul wanted to see that purpose realized in his life. For that to happen, however, Paul would have many difficulties to face. He was willing to do that in order to become all that Jesus intended him to be.

How many of us will actually reach our potential for Christ? How many times have we fallen short of the purpose that Christ has for us? It is true that without the Lord Jesus and his Spirit, we could do nothing. The work of becoming more like Christ and reaching the purpose he has for us is a cooperative effort between the Spirit of God and each of us. I can resist what God is doing in my life. I can choose to live in disobedience for a time. I can delay in doing what he is asking me to do. Many believers live their lives without ever reaching their potential. They allow fear to stop them. Some are content where they are. Paul challenges us to press on. He challenges us to know Christ and his power in a deeper way. We can only do this by remaining faithful. To reach our potential we must be ready to face the battle. We must, like Paul, be willing to suffer if necessary. There is no easy way.

Again in verse 13 Paul tells us that he had not yet taken hold of the goal for which Christ had saved him. There was still more work to be done in his life. There was still more that the Lord Jesus wanted to accomplish through and in him. Knowing this, Paul told the Philippians that he forgot what was behind and strained toward what was ahead. There are two things we need to see here.

Notice that Paul tells us that he forgot what was behind. The first step in pushing ahead is to let go of the past. You cannot move ahead if you are tied to the past. For some of us, this will mean forgiving those who have offended us. Resentment binds us to the past and keeps us from moving forward.

Forgetting the past means not only forgiving others but also accepting Christ's forgiveness ourselves. We have all failed Christ at one time or another. We have all done things that we are ashamed to admit. Often these things can keep us from moving ahead. Our past failures make us unwilling to move forward in service. We live defeated lives. We fear that we might fail again. We feel unworthy of accepting a new ministry because of our past. If there is one thing we know about the apostle Paul, it is that he remembered his past and his persecution of the church. He called himself the least of the apostles because he had at one time persecuted the church (1 Corinthians 15:9). Forgetting the past for Paul meant that he had to accept the forgiveness of Christ for all he had done to the church. How easy it would have been for him to live in a sense of unworthiness and defeat! He had caused so much harm to the church. Satan would have delighted in keeping Paul in this place of defeat. Paul refused to remain there, however. He pressed on. He refused to live in defeat over what he had done. He accepted the forgiveness of the Lord and moved on.

Forgetting what is behind also means not dwelling on our past successes. It would have been possible for Paul to spend his time focusing on all the great and wonderful things that God had done in and through him. There are pastors and Christian workers who never advance because they get stuck on some past success. To press on is to thank God for the successes of the past but not to dwell on them. You can't move ahead if you can't get beyond the successes of the past. There is more work to be done. God is not finished with you. Don't stop after you have seen God do one great thing through you. Press on. Put these successes out of your mind and move ahead. Don't let the success of the past cloud your mind and keep you from seeing what God has for you in the future.

Paul's focus was to press forward. He would not let the past keep him from the blessings of the future. He was not going to give up. He was going to take advantage of the time the Lord had given him. In this last lap of the race of life, Paul was going to push himself even harder. He had already accomplished much, but he was not going to let that keep him from pushing forward even more. As long as he had not reached the goal of perfect maturity, he would keep running the race before him.

In verse 15 Paul told the Philippians that every mature believer should have this attitude. The sign of maturity is this healthy desire to know Christ even more. Mature Christians recognize that they still need to grow in Christ. The mature Christian is one who is able to put the past aside and press on into the future. A mature believer will not let past failures or successes hinder future service. Paul trusted God to reveal this truth in a deeper way to those who struggled with it in Philippi (see verse 15).

Paul concluded his thoughts on this matter in verse 16 by challenging the Philippians to live up to the divine knowledge they had already attained. What lessons has God already taught you in life? How many times do we have to learn the same lessons over and over again? There are times that instead of moving ahead I seem to move backwards. There are times when I do not seem even to be able to live the lessons I have already learned. God has brought each of us to a certain point in our spiritual journey, and yet we often live below that level. He has stretched our faith in certain areas, and yet when we come to another obstacle, we don't seem to be able to trust him. He has taught us to walk, yet we still crawl. He demonstrated his power and opened wonderful doors for us, yet we fail to trust him to do what he has already shown us he can do. If we are going to press on, we need to begin by remembering the lessons God has already taught us.

For Consideration:

• Do you know Christ now? Do you have a passion to know him more? To what extent would you go to know him more?

- What does this passage teach us about reaching our potential for Christ? Have you reached your full potential for Christ? How much more do you think Christ could do in you and through you?

- What things do you need to forget in order to advance spiritually? Are there failures that you need to forget? Are there people you need to forgive?

- Have you been able to live up to what you have already attained in Christ? Does he have to teach you the same lesson over and over again? Explain.

For Prayer:

- Ask the Lord to increase your desire to know him more. Ask him to forgive you for not pressing on.

- Ask the Lord to allow you to live in the power of his resurrection with victory over sin and death.

- Thank the Lord that he has forgiven you of your past failures. Ask him to give you a greater boldness to move forward now.

- Ask the Lord to give you grace to live out the lessons he has been teaching you.

9

Enemies of
the Cross

Read Philippians 3:17–21

In the last section we saw how Paul expressed his deep desire to press on in his spiritual growth. In this section he challenged the Philippians to follow his example.

We need to understand that Paul realized he still had far to go in his journey to perfect righteousness. He did not invite others to follow his example because he had everything in order in his life. He was the first to admit that he had not yet arrived. This is very clear in his earlier statement in this chapter: "Not that I have already obtained all this, or have already been made perfect, but I press on to take hold of that for which Christ Jesus took hold of me. Brothers, I do not consider myself yet to have taken hold of it. But one thing I do: Forgetting what is behind and straining toward what is ahead, I press on toward the goal to win the prize for which God has called me heavenward in Christ Jesus" (verses 12–14).

What Paul was telling the Philippians to do was to adopt

his attitude of pressing on to be more like Christ. Paul knew that he was not yet fully mature, but he was still striving to imitate Christ. When it comes to our spiritual growth, there is really only one person we can truly follow: the Lord Jesus. He alone lived a perfect life free from sin. If we become followers of any other person, we will fall short. Paul understood this when he told the Philippians to follow his example. He wanted the Philippians to imitate him as far as he imitated Christ. In his letter to Timothy, he had this to say about himself: "Here is a trustworthy saying that deserves full acceptance: Christ Jesus came into the world to save sinners—of whom I am the worst" (1 Timothy 1:15). Notice how he considers himself to be the worst of all sinners. He had no delusions about his human perfection. Paul knew he was a sinner. He wrestled with the same things we wrestle with today. Again, in Romans 7:14–15 Paul wrote: "We know that the law is spiritual; but I am unspiritual, sold as a slave to sin. I do not understand what I do. For what I want to do I do not do, but what I hate I do."

There was one thing, however, that Paul did have that we need to have: a burning desire to know the Lord Jesus and to become everything Jesus wanted him to be. No, he wasn't perfect, but he was pressing on toward perfection. We should not set ourselves up as examples to follow in all things. What we can do, however, is adopt the attitude of Paul in pressing on in godly service to Christ. People will not see perfection in us, but they should see this desire to press on. They should see that we are growing in our love for Christ and others; this was what Paul was asking the Philippians to follow.

Paul reminded the Philippians that they would have to deal with the enemies of the cross as they pressed on to know the Lord Jesus. In verse 17 Paul told the Philippians to take note of those who were living according to the pattern that the Lord Jesus had given to them and follow their godly examples.

It grieved the heart of Paul that many individuals lived as enemies of the cross (verse 18). It would be very easy to think that all these individuals were outside of the church, but Paul seems to be speaking here about individuals who had already come in among them. Could it be that these were the people Paul mentioned earlier in this epistle who were teaching the error that circumcision was necessary for salvation? Whoever these individuals were, they were a real threat.

Paul described these individuals in verse 19. Firstly, he wrote that the enemies of Christ were on a path that led to final destruction. A judgment was coming, and they were heading straight for that judgment. One day as they rounded the bend in their earthly lives, they would come face to face with a holy God. They would look up and realize that their end had come. They would be judged for what they had done against the church and the devastation they had caused.

Secondly, Paul told the Philippians that the god of these enemies of the cross was their stomach. This means that their only concern was to satisfy their personal appetites. Their desire was to fill their stomachs and their lives with the good things of this world. Their goal in life was to get whatever they could for themselves. They were governed by their lusts and passions. They were ruled by their physical needs and desires. They were not concerned about spiritual matters. Paul told his readers that the minds of these enemies of the cross were only on earthly matters.

Finally, Paul told the Philippians that the glory of these enemies of the cross was in their shame. What did these individuals boast about? They boasted about their accomplishments. They boasted of their wealth. They boasted about their wild parties and sinful desires. I spend a lot of time writing in coffee shops. There are times when I cannot help but overhear the conversations of those around me. I hear people boasting of how much beer they drank the night before. They boast of their sexual adventures and their immoral lifestyles. They ought to feel shame about these things, but they don't. They boast of things that will ultimately bring them shame.

Those who truly belonged to Christ were very different. These individuals followed the example of Paul in pressing on to know Christ. Their citizenship was in heaven. They longed for the return of the Lord Jesus who would transform their bodies so that they would be like him. They would be free from the lusts and passions of this earthly body. In these new bodies, they would enter into the physical presence of Christ to live forever. This was their greatest delight. They eagerly waited for the Lord to come and transform them. In the meantime, however, they continued to press on to glorify him in their frail and weak earthly bodies.

We need to see the contrast in this passage. On the one hand were the enemies of the cross. These individuals sought the things of this world. They filled their stomachs and filled their lives with all that this world had to offer them. They delighted in being respected and honored by those around them. Their minds were on the things of this earth.

On the other hand were those who pressed on to know the Lord. They removed their eyes from this world and focused them on the Lord Jesus. The things of this world appeared empty and hollow to them. Their delight and desires were in the Lord Jesus alone, who filled them and satisfied them in ways that nothing in this world ever could.

There are still these two types of people in this world: those who seek this world and those who seek the Savior. We all fall into one of these categories. Where do you fall today?

For Consideration:

• Paul described two types of people in this passage. What are they? Which type most closely resembles you?

- To what extent does your desire to know the Lord Jesus influence your personal life?

- Who alone is our perfect example? Are there other people who have been an example of "pressing on" for you personally? Explain.

- Paul was an example of "pressing on." To what extent is your life an example of this?

For Prayer:

- Ask the Lord to renew your desire to know him and experience him.

- Ask the Lord to forgive you for the times when your focus has been taken from him and placed on the things of this world.

- Ask the Lord to show you any area of your life that keeps you from growing in the Lord.

- Thank the Lord Jesus that he gave us the one perfect example that we can truly follow.

10

Stand Firm

Read Philippians 4:1–9

I n the last few meditations, we saw how Paul encouraged
the Philippians to press on in their relationship with the
Lord. He encouraged them to set Jesus as their example
in all they did. They would not be perfect in this life, but they
were to give themselves to becoming more and more like the
Lord Jesus.

Here in this section Paul challenged the Philippians in
some very particular areas of their Christian life. First, he
reaffirmed his relationship with them. He told them that
he loved them and longed for them. He missed being with
them. The believers in Philippi were a special blessing to
Paul. He considered them to be his great joy and crown. For
an athlete the crown was a symbol of victory. Paul valued
the Philippians as his crown and symbol of success. He took
great joy in them and their relationship with the Lord.

If the Philippians were going to stand firm and become
all the Lord wanted them to become, there were several

things that needed to happen. Let's consider each subject addressed by Paul in this passage.

Relationships

Paul began by commanding two of the members of the church to learn how to agree with each other; he even mentioned their names. Obviously, Euodia and Syntyche were having problems getting along. This problem was affecting the work of the Lord in this assembly. Notice that these women had contended with Paul in the cause of the gospel. Paul recognized them as co-workers and true believers. While they were servants of the gospel, they were having problems with each other. We are not told what their problems were, but they were significant enough to break the fellowship between the two women. Paul encouraged the church of Philippi to help these women. He does not tell us how he expected the church to help.

It is interesting to note that Paul challenged these women to agree with each other "in the Lord" (verse 2). What does Paul mean? Let's face it—there are many areas of life where we will never completely agree with our brothers and sisters in the Lord. Some of us prefer a certain style of worship while others prefer another. There are many ways in which we differ in the body of Christ, and these differences can be healthy. God is not calling us to agree with everyone in all things. He is calling us to agree "in the Lord," however. When we speak of agreeing "in the Lord," we speak of agreeing on those things that the Lord wants us to agree on. This means recognizing that though our brother or sister differs from us in style, preference, and understanding of minor doctrinal issues, we are still brothers and sisters in the Lord. While we may not always see things in the same way, we do need to love and respect each other. God calls us to join our hands and unite in those key areas where he has called us to be one and to work together for his sake. We are not speaking here about those who deny the fundamental truths of the faith. Paul is speaking here about two women who loved the Lord and served him. How often have we let small differences of personality and preference divide us? Preferences should never divide the body of Christ. All too often, we spend our time fighting over minor issues. There comes a time when we need to learn how to put aside these differences and agree to respect each other. This is what Paul is calling for in the church of Philippi.

The church of our day has divided over small issues. We often emphasize our differences. One church baptizes infants and another baptizes only believing adults. One believes that we must honor God by a quiet and reverent worship style while others feel free to celebrate with clapping their hands and dancing. The list of things that can divide us is endless. If we are going to stand firm, we will have to learn how to deal with our differences and learn how to work with each other. How often have insignificant differences between true believers hindered the work of the Lord? It is time for us to recognize that the Lord blesses those who differ from us in style of worship or minor theological issues. Instead of spending our time arguing with other believers, we need to agree with the Lord and learn to work together for the sake of his kingdom.

Rejoicing

The second matter that Paul brings to the Philippians is the matter of rejoicing. To Paul joy and rejoicing were key ingredients in the Christian life. Listen to what Paul told the Romans: "For the kingdom of God is not a matter of eating and drinking, but of righteousness, peace and joy in the Holy Spirit" (Romans 14:17). For Paul the kingdom of God could be summarized by three words: righteousness, peace, and joy. It is interesting that Paul saw joy as being so important.

Notice that Paul told the Philippians that they were to

rejoice in the Lord always. He repeated this for emphasis in verse 4. The rejoicing that Paul is speaking about here is a rejoicing in the Lord. Paul is not telling us to rejoice in the evil we see around us. He is not even calling us to rejoice in the trials we face. He is telling us here, however, to rejoice in the Lord. What a difference it makes when we know the Lord. We can be joyful because he is Lord and will work out all things for our good. We can be joyful because he cares for us no matter what we face. While we may not take great joy in our pain and suffering, we do rejoice in the fact that we are in the hands of a powerful God who loves us deeply. When we get our eyes off our pain and suffering and on the Lord, there is much reason to rejoice.

There is a connection here between standing firm and rejoicing in the Lord. It is the heart of God that we learn to rejoice in him. Our relationship with the Lord Jesus ought to be exciting. The only way we can stand firm in the Lord is to learn how to look to him beyond the problems we face. When we learn how to rejoice in Christ and his purposes for us, what a difference it makes to our worship and service. We do not honor the Lord Jesus by coming to him with a heart that is not rejoicing. It is the heart of God that I live in the joy of my salvation. While my circumstance may change, the Lord Jesus will not change. His purpose and love for me will always remain. In this I can rejoice. While I may not be able to rejoice in my suffering and pain, I can rejoice in the fact that my Savior is bigger than them all. I can rejoice in his promises and provision. A rejoicing Christian has a powerful witness in the world, showing the world that God is real.

Gentleness

In verse 5 Paul challenged the believers to let their gentleness be evident to all. This gentleness was not only to be demonstrated to their friends and loved ones but also to their enemies. The word *all* includes everyone.

Gentleness is a quality that accepts with grace whatever comes. The Lord Jesus demonstrated this gentleness when he was being accused and beaten. He responded with tenderness toward his enemies. When Stephen was being stoned, he pleaded with the Lord not to hold his enemies responsible for what they were doing (Acts 7:59–60). Gentleness does not seek revenge. Gentleness responds with blessing to all who would seek harm. Gentleness means forgiving, caring, and demonstrating great patience with those who offend.

Notice that Paul told the Philippians that they were to be gentle because the Lord was near. This means that the Lord was near to them in their suffering. He was near to them when their enemies were insulting or persecuting them. Being near to them, the Lord saw what was happening. He would not ignore what they were suffering. He would care for them and deal with those who offended them. It was not for them to seek revenge. It was for them to live in obedience and respond in love and gentleness. They did not need to respond in any other way because God would judge evil and would care for them.

Resisting Anxiety

In verse 6 Paul told the Philippians that they were not to be anxious about anything. Very often we become anxious when we feel that things are out of our control. We become anxious because we do not know what the next hours will bring. As children of God, however, we are to learn how to present all our requests, burdens, and needs to the Lord in prayer. We are to realize that he is a big and loving God, and we are his children. We are to put all our needs in his hands and trust him with them. Notice that Paul told the Philippians that they were to pray and petition the Lord with thanksgiving (see verse 6). We all are to do this because we know that he will care for us. What do we have to fear if we are in the hands of God? Is he big enough to take care of our needs? Does he not call us to present our needs to him? Does he not love us as his very own children?

Paul told them that if they simply presented their needs to the Lord and learned to trust him, then the peace of God would fill their hearts. That peace would guard their hearts and minds in Christ Jesus. How often has anxiety caused us to lose our joy and peace? How often has anxiety caused us to fret and worry for nothing? Sometimes this anxiety will take our attention from the Lord Jesus. Our minds become filled with unbelief and distrust. If you want to protect your heart and mind from evil, you need to let them be filled with the peace of God. When you find yourself becoming anxious, you need to take the time to commit your problems and needs to the Lord. You need to take all these problems and leave them at his feet. You need to wait on him until his peace fills your heart and protects you. How often has anxiety destroyed our testimony as believers? Paul calls us to banish it from our lives and to trust in God our Father who will care for us in all our needs.

The Thought Life

There is another thing that Paul challenged the Philippians to do. In verse 8 he challenged them to banish negative thoughts from their minds. Instead, they were to think on those things that were true, noble, right, pure, lovely, admirable, excellent, and praiseworthy. The unholy thoughts and images we allow into our minds and hearts will remain there and cause problems for us. What kind of things are you letting into your mind? What kind of things are you reading? If you have a television, what kind of things are you watching? If you fill your mind with evil thoughts and attitudes, will this not become evident in your life? Your body and your mind are the temple of the Holy Spirit.

What kind of thoughts and attitudes are you letting into that temple?

Paul tells us in verse 8 that instead of allowing evil into our hearts, we are to think on those things that are pure, excellent, and praiseworthy. Instead of being negative and critical toward your brothers and sisters in Christ, seek to find their good qualities. If you plant evil thoughts in your mind, what kind of fruit would you expect to find? If, on the other hand, you plant pure and excellent thoughts and images, will this not affect your actions and relationships as well?

Following Paul's Example

Beyond these very practical matters, Paul challenged the Philippians to put into practice those things they had learned from him. This related not only to the truth that Paul had taught them but also to the truth he had demonstrated in his own life while he was with them. Paul had confidence that he had lived well among the Philippians. His desire was not only to teach the truth but also to live it out before them. He reminded the Philippians in verse 9 that as they sought to put these things into practice, the God of peace would be with them. He would strengthen and equip them so that they could become all that God had called them to be.

Paul was immensely practical in this last section. For Paul the Christian life was not just about doctrine and truth; it was also about living in a very real world. The Christian life is about dealing with people who are different from us in many ways. It is about learning how to live in joy, despite the obstacles that come our way. It is about learning how to banish anxiety and live in the gentleness of the Spirit, knowing that God will care for us. The biggest challenge in the Christian life is not about getting the right doctrine but about learning how to put that doctrine into practice in our everyday life. When the unbelieving world looks at us, they are not interested in what we say we believe. They are more interested in how we live in light of the doctrine we profess.

Are you a believer today? Is this evident in your relationships with those around you? Is it evident in the joy you have in serving and knowing the Lord? Is it evident in your positive attitude and gentleness in the midst of suffering and trial? When Paul challenged the Philippians to stand firm, he was challenging them to learn how to live their faith in real life.

For Consideration:

• Are there believers you have problems with today? Will believers ever completely agree with each other? What does Paul challenge us to do here about these relationships?

• How much are you rejoicing in the Lord today? What stands in the way of your experiencing an even greater joy in the Lord?

• What makes you anxious in life? What does Paul challenge you to do with these anxieties?

• Take a look at what kind of thoughts you are allowing into your mind today. What do you need to do with these negative attitudes and thoughts?

For Prayer:

• Ask the Lord to help you to rejoice more in him.

• Take a moment to bring your anxieties to the Lord. Ask him to fill you with his peace and the knowledge that he will care for you.

- Are there people around you who mistreat you or speak evil of you? Ask the Lord to give you a gentle spirit toward them.

- Take a moment to pray for another church in your community. Thank the Lord for them and ask him to truly bless them in their ministry.

11

Content in Every Situation

Read Philippians 4:10–23

I n this final section of the epistle to the Philippians, Paul expressed his gratitude to the Philippians for their support and encouragement in his time of need. Paul knew what it was like to be in need. Even though he served the Lord, there were many times when he lived in severe physical hardship. He understood need. This gave him a deeper appreciation for the gifts the Philippians sent to him.

In verse 10 Paul told the Philippians that he greatly rejoiced in the fact that they had renewed their involvement in his circumstances. They were always concerned for him, but they had not always had an opportunity to demonstrate their interest. Very likely, this renewed concern was demonstrated in the form of a gift that came through Epaphroditus (see verse 18). Paul was now sending him back to Philippi because he had been sick (see 2:25). Paul deeply appreciated this gift from the Philippian church.

In verse 11 Paul told the church that he was not looking

for a gift from them. He had learned to be content in whatever situation he found himself. He was quite satisfied to continue as he was, but this gift certainly made things much easier for him. And for this he was very thankful.

There were individuals in ministry in Paul's day who demanded wages. They expected that wherever they went, the people of God would shower them with blessings. Even in our day, there are pastors who choose whether they will go to a certain church by how much money they will get. Paul refused to let money be the factor that determined whether he would live in obedience. He would go wherever God sent him, whether there was money in it or not. He had to learn how to be content to live in whatever situation he found himself. If he had to go hungry for a time, Paul was willing to do this. He did not complain about his lot in life. In the last meditation, we saw how Paul challenged the Philippians to be anxious for nothing. Instead, they were to bring all their requests to the Lord and trust in his purposes and provision.

True contentment can only come when we are surrendered to the will and purpose of God. Contentment is the fruit of accepting God's purposes for us in whatever state we find ourselves. It is the result of trusting God and believing that his purposes are for our good and the expansion of his kingdom.

For Paul, God controlled not only the good times but the difficult times as well. Paul knew what it was like to be in need. There were times when he went hungry. He also knew what it was like to be living in plenty. He had to learn how to be content in both these circumstances. Paul was able to rejoice in every situation because he had strength that came from the Lord Jesus. He reminded the Philippians that he did this through Christ who gave him strength. This contentment was a gift from God to Paul.

Some might think that it would be easy to be content in prosperity, but the reality of the matter is that sometimes those who live in plenty have more struggle being content than those who have very little. Often, the more we have, the more we want. The more that surrounds us, the more we want of it. Those who live in prosperity also have to learn to be content.

Contentment is very important in the Christian life. Let us take a moment to consider the result of a lack of contentment. Lack of contentment can lead to dishonesty, anger, and even fighting. It is the fertile soil in which jealousy and anger grow. It is the reason why countries have gone to war. It is the cause of murder, theft, and violence of all kinds. Discontent can take control of individuals and become their god. Their lives become focused on seeking more and more. Eventually, dissatisfaction will destroy all it conquers. Paul had learned the art of being content. How important it is that we learn, like Paul, to be satisfied. Discontentment rejects the will and purpose of God and seeks its own pleasure and its own way.

Paul was not saying that he did not appreciate the gift the Philippians sent him. On the contrary, Paul had learned to receive gifts from God's people. It was not his desire to refuse any good thing that God might give him, but he was not in constant pursuit of material things.

Paul recognized that the believers in Philippi had been a tremendous blessing to him throughout his ministry. They had shared what they had with him when no other church did. They had never forgotten the apostle. Paul reminded them of how they had given to him when he left Macedonia. In verse 16 he wrote that in Thessalonica he had received over and over again from Philippi. Once again, the church in Philippi had sent a gift through Epaphroditus (see verse 18). These gifts were fragrant offerings to God. Paul knew that in giving to him, the church of Philippi was giving to God. God would not let this go unnoticed. Paul rejoiced in the fact that this gift would be credited to the account of the Philippians in heaven.

Paul knew that while these believers had to sacrifice to give this gift, God would meet their needs. As they reached out in obedience to meet the needs of those around them, God would also provide for them. There is a principle here that we need to see.

God gives to us so we can give to those who need it. It is true that we have needs also. God provides for those needs as well. Our resources, however, are not ours to store and use as we please. We must commit all we have to the Lord and be open to his leading regarding how he would have us use those resources. The promise of God is that if we use our resources as God directs, he will take care of us in our hour of need. This is the clear teaching of the Scriptures. The writer of Ecclesiastes tells us: "Cast your bread upon the waters, for after many days you will find it again" (Ecclesiastes 11:1). This same thought is repeated in the Proverbs 11:25: "A generous man will prosper; he who refreshes others will himself be refreshed."

There are those who would take this instruction and use it to teach that if we give we will get *more* in return. They teach that we need to sow our money like a farmer sows his field. They claim that if you want to get rich, this is how you need to live. They encourage individuals to give in order that they will receive more in return.

We need to be careful of this teaching for several reasons. First, if we teach that we are to give in order to receive more in return, we can encourage greed and discontent. What Paul is telling us here is that we need to learn to be content in whatever situation we find ourselves. To encourage people to give in order that they will receive material blessing in return is to encourage discontent. It is to focus attention on the things of this earth and not on spiritual matters.

Second, this teaching does not fit the life of Christ and

the apostles. No one gave more than the Lord Jesus, yet he tells us that he did not even have as much as a place to lay his head. In Luke 9:58 Jesus stated: "Foxes have holes and birds of the air have nests, but the Son of Man has no place to lay his head." Paul himself tells us that there were times when he went hungry. The whole context of this passage is one of learning how to be content not only in prosperity but also in poverty.

The last thing we need to see here is that often when we teach people to give in order to receive in return, we create a real problem regarding the motive behind giving. When Jesus gave he did so in a selfless way. In other words, he gave not expecting to receive in return. If the only reason we give is to receive something in return, we are not giving to the Lord but to ourselves.

Having given these warnings, the truth remains. By giving to the cause of Christ, the church of Philippi was blessed. They were laying up treasures in heaven. If God is leading you to give and putting needs on your heart, don't hesitate to obey. He knows what he is doing. Live in obedience and God will take care of you in your need. The key here is to be obedient to God in the use of your resources. Paul had seen this in his own life, and for this he gives glory to the Lord, his provider (see verse 20).

Paul concluded his letter with some personal greetings from the brothers who were with him (verse 21). Special greetings came from the servants of Caesar's household. These were quite likely those who had been converted during Paul's stay as a prisoner. God had a purpose for Paul. Even in his imprisonment, Paul was being used by God to reach souls for his kingdom. Paul was content in his imprisonment, for he had found the Lord's purpose.

Paul has much to teach us in this passage about contentment. We are to give out of a heart that is satisfied and joyful. We are to seek God in every circumstance we

find ourselves. Paul learned the art of contentment—have
we?

For Consideration:

- Those who are content have been able to see God in
  their situation and have surrendered to his purpose. Do
  you agree with this definition? How does this relate to
  where you find yourself today?

- Why is contentment so important? Where does
  discontentment lead?

- Why is it important to deal with the attitude of giving so
  that we can receive in return?

- How do you find the balance between giving in order to
  receive and giving out of obedience and trusting God for
  your needs? What is the difference between the two?

For Prayer:

- Are you content with where you are now? Ask God to
  teach you how to be content.

- Ask God to give you a heart that is willing to listen and
  give when he moves you to give.

- Thank God that he has entrusted you with his resources.
  Ask him to forgive you for thinking that these resources
  were yours alone.

Colossians

12

The Faith and Love of the Colossians

Read Colossians 1:1–12

This is a letter from the apostle Paul to the believers in Colosse. Notice how Paul sent his greetings to them from Timothy as well. The mention of Timothy here shows us something of the relationship between Paul and Timothy. Some believe that Timothy acted as Paul's secretary. Paul was in prison when he wrote this letter. In this first section of the letter, Paul commended the Colossians for their faith and love.

Notice as we begin that Paul declared himself to be an apostle of Christ Jesus by the will of God. This was not a position that Paul had sought for himself. There were many in those days who wanted to be apostles. Many declared themselves to have this office in the church, but they were false apostles. The Lord had a specific purpose for Paul. He did not have to go searching for that position or office; it was given to him by God. I have met many individuals who have sought positions and offices in the church. I have also met individuals who have received those positions by God. If you are seeking the will of the Lord, God will reveal that place to you. It will be evident to all around you that this position has been given to you by God, who will open the doors. He will bless what he has called you to do. Paul knew he was an apostle because the Lord had made that very clear to Paul and to all who came in contact with him.

Paul sent his greetings to the Colossians. Notice in verse 2 what he said about these believers. He called them "holy and faithful brothers." This says something about the church in Colosse. It was a holy church, set apart for God and his purposes. Not only was it consecrated to God, but it was also faithful. Here was a church that had remained true to the gospel and had a testimony of being holy and faithful. Paul commended this.

Paul told the Colossians that when he prayed for them, he always thanked God for them because he had heard of their faith and love for the saints (verse 3). They not only loved each other but also all other fellow believers. The Colossians were known for their love. What a powerful testimony this was! Paul took some time to examine this faith and love of the Colossians. He told them that both faith and love sprang from the hope that was stored up in heaven through the message of the gospel. Let's examine what Paul was saying here.

Faith and love spring from hope that is stored up for us in heaven. What is this hope? Our hope as believers is the forgiveness of our sins through the Lord Jesus Christ and his work on the cross. Our hope is that through this forgiveness we will one day enter the presence of God and live forever with him, free from the effects of sin. Our hope is that we will live in perfect communion and fellowship with our Creator.

If this is the hope we have, how does this produce faith and love in us? As we look to what the Lord Jesus has done for us, we are strengthened in our faith. Trials may come but as we look to heaven, we are strengthened in our resolve. We are able to face our trials because we know that heaven is our home. Whatever happens to us here is not the end. Imagine where you would be today in your spiritual journey if you did not have the assurance of this hope in heaven. Where would you be if you could not look to up to heaven and see that your name is in the book of life? Does our hope in heaven not strengthen us in our faith here below?

This hope in heaven also strengthens us in our love. The hope we have relates to the forgiveness of the Lord Jesus. He reached out to us and loved us just as we were. Knowing that we are loved and that Jesus has prepared a place in heaven for us encourages us to love him in return. It also encourages us to love one another, as he commanded. Those who have come to know the Lord Jesus and the hope he has for them, naturally love in return. We can love because he first loved us. We can love because the hope we have fills us with love for others. Love springs from what Jesus has done for us and the hope we have in heaven.

Notice also in verse 5 that this hope is communicated to us by means of the truth of the gospel. We would never have known about this wonderful hope if we had not heard the message of the gospel, which told us the good news of a Savior who came to save a sinful world. What incredible truth the gospel brings to us! We have hope by means of the gospel. There are many people who have never heard this message and the hope that they can have in the Lord Jesus. It is for us to tell them.

Paul reminded the Colossians that this simple message of the gospel was bearing fruit all over the world. The message of the gospel is not a complicated message. It uncovers, however, the treasures of heaven and the news of the forgiveness of sin to those who will listen. Those who believe this truth and accept it are radically changed. The gospel is able to bear fruit in fertile hearts. Wherever there is a heart that is open to receive the truth of the gospel, this simple message will do its work and transform that life. The light appears and the darkness is chased away. Life begins to make sense. There is meaning and purpose to existence. The believers in Colosse had heard this message, and it literally transformed their lives. The seed of the gospel produced the fruit of faith and love in their hearts.

In verse 7 Paul tells us that the Colossians heard this simple message of the gospel from a servant by the name of Epaphras. Paul commended this man as a faithful minister of the gospel. It was through Epaphras that Paul had heard of the faith and love of the Colossians.

What we need to see here is the power of the simple gospel. Epaphras preached that gospel in Colosse. The result was a powerful work of the Spirit of God to transform the city. The secret of the success of Epaphras's ministry was that he shared the simple truth. It was the gospel that was empowered by the Holy Spirit to produce a change in the hearts and lives of the Colossians. This simple message has the power to change. This message chases away darkness and opens the eyes of the spiritually blind. We dare not underestimate the power of this simple message. It changed the city of Colosse and many towns and cities like it.

When Paul heard of the faith and love of the Colossians, he began to pray for them. Notice what he prayed for the Colossians. Paul prayed that God would fill them with the knowledge of his will through spiritual wisdom and understanding. It was wonderful that God had saved the Colossians, but salvation was only the beginning. Next they needed to seek the will and purpose of God in their salvation. God had saved them for a purpose that they needed to know and fulfill. Why has God saved you? What is his purpose for you as his child? What gifts has he given you? Where does he want you to serve him now? These were the questions that needed to be answered by the Colossians after they came to know God's plan of salvation through the gospel. Paul prayed that God would give them wisdom to know his will and purpose.

Notice that this knowledge was not a natural knowledge. Paul told the Colossians that he was praying that God would fill them with spiritual knowledge and understanding. There is a world of difference between natural and spiritual wisdom and understanding. Paul's prayer was that the Colossians would put aside their own interests and goals in life. He was praying that God would give them a knowledge and understanding that did not come from themselves but from the Spirit of God. He was praying that they would have the mind of God regarding his purpose and plan for them.

Paul also prayed that the Colossians would live lives that were worthy of the Lord Jesus, pleasing God in every way (verse 10). Paul went on to explain how they could please God. First, they would please God by bearing fruit. It is the will and purpose of God that his children bring others to Christ and live a godly life. God delights to see us using our spiritual gifts for his glory. If you want to please God in every way, you will need to grow in the gifts he has given you to bear fruit for his kingdom.

Second, Paul wrote that pleasing God in every way involved growing in knowledge of God. This can be accomplished in two different ways: by seeking him in the Scriptures and by experiencing him in obedience to his word. It is a good thing to study the Bible for the purpose of knowing more about God, but if you don't experience the reality of the truth in your daily life, you really don't know God at all. You can read about the love of God and know it in your mind, but you really don't know his love until you also experience it in real life. You can read about how God empowers believers in service and provides for their every need, but you really don't know this until you have experienced it personally. To grow in the knowledge of God is to not only understand the truth about him but also to experience him in real life.

Third, Paul told the Colossians that if they were to please God in every way, they would need to be strengthened by his power (verse 11). They needed his power for three reasons: endurance, patience, and giving thanks. They needed to be strengthened so that they would have great endurance. The life of service God had called them to was not going to be easy. There would be difficulties and trials along the way. If they wanted to please God in every way, they would need to be strengthened in order to endure hardship to the end.

They also needed to be strengthened in order to have patience. Patience is the ability to remain under a load. When the pressure mounted and things began to get difficult, the Colossians would need to have great patience to remain under that pressure until the Lord set them free. It would be in those times of pressure that they would be shaped and strengthened. Paul prayed that the Colossians would not run away from their problems but let those problems strengthen them in their devotion and commitment to Christ. If you are a Christian, you will face opposition. If you want to please God in every way, you will let that opposition strengthen you. You will not run from it but remain faithful in it.

The Colossians would also need to be strengthened in order to joyfully give thanks to God. Joy would not be an easy emotion to maintain. When things got difficult, the natural tendency would be to grumble and complain. But if they wanted to please God in every way, they needed to be a thankful people. No one can please God by murmuring and doubting.

Paul concluded this section by reminding the Colossians that they had much to be thankful for. He told them in verse 12 that God had qualified them to share in the inheritance of the kingdom of saints. They did not qualify in themselves but in Christ. The Lord Jesus came to offer forgiveness for sin. When we accept what God offers in his Son, we become his children. As his forgiven children, we are qualified to be inheritors of his kingdom of light. What a privilege we have to be inheritors of the kingdom of heaven. We have every reason to be thankful, even if here below so many things seem to go against us.

For Consideration:

• How is our faith strengthened by the hope we have? Give an example.

• What do we learn here about the power of the simple gospel?

• What was the particular purpose of God in saving you? What has he called you to do?

• What trials has God called you to endure as a believer? How has he strengthened you to endure and be patient in these trials?

For Prayer:

• Thank the Lord for the hope he has given you in heaven.

• Ask God to make his purpose and plan for your life very clear.

• Ask God to increase your joy and thankfulness.

• Ask God to enable you to know him not only intellectually but also in experience.

13

He Is

Read Colossians 1:13–20

In the last meditation, Paul spoke to the Colossians and reminded them of his prayer for them. He prayed that they would move from the salvation they had experienced to growth and fruitfulness. This was their only reasonable response to the Lord for what he had done for them. In this next section of chapter 1, Paul reminded the Colossians of what the Lord Jesus had done for them. In particular, he emphasized who Jesus is.

Paul began by recalling what the Lord Jesus had done for the Colossians. He told them in verse 13 that the Lord God had rescued them from the "dominion of darkness." This darkness was Satan's kingdom of sin and rebellion against God. There are many who are trapped in this realm of evil today. They are bound by the cords of sin's slavery. They live for this world and its pleasures and cannot see the reality of the Lord Jesus and the hope he brings. They need to be rescued from this kingdom because all who belong to it will one day be judged by God.

Paul spoke of the dominion of darkness. The word *dominion* is quite important. In the Greek language it can mean "power, authority or control." Paul was telling the Colossians that at one time demonic darkness had controlled them. They had been trapped under its power and authority. This leads us to understand that it had been impossible for them to get free from this evil power in their own strength. They had remained under sin's domination and control until someone came and rescued them. They had been in a serious situation. They had been unable to free themselves from sin and darkness, and they were hopelessly bound for God's judgment—unless something happened.

Paul reminded the Colossians that it was the Lord Jesus who rescued them from the power of darkness and God's eternal punishment. Christ broke the power of evil and set them free from its chains. The Lord God brought them "into the kingdom of the Son he loves." Notice that believers are brought into the kingdom of the Son. We are brought into the same kingdom as the Lord Jesus, whom the Father loves. This reveals something about how the Lord God feels toward us. He has adopted us and placed us in the kingdom of his own Son. We become heirs with Christ Jesus of eternity and intimacy with God.

Through the Lord Jesus we have received many blessings. Paul tells us in verse 14 that we have received redemption and forgiveness of sin. When something is redeemed, it is bought back. Because of sin we were enemies of God and inhabitants of the kingdom of darkness. The Lord Jesus rescued us from that kingdom of darkness at the cost of his life. He paid the ultimate price so that we could become children of God, clothed with forgiveness. We were sinners and rebels against God, but now all that has been forgiven. Christ took our punishment on himself, satisfying the demands of justice. We are clean as we stand before the Father, as if we had never sinned. We do not deserve this mercy, but it is freely offered to us. Now when the Lord God looks down on us, he sees us as his children, cleansed by the forgiveness that Jesus has brought. God will never hold our sins against us because they have been paid for by his Son.

Paul proclaimed Jesus to be "the image of the invisible God" (verse 15). An image is a representation or exact likeness of something else. In this case, Paul tells us that Jesus is a visible demonstration of the invisible God. In other words, when Jesus came to live among us, he showed us exactly who God is. When we look at Christ, we see the Father. We see the characteristics of the Father in the Son. We see the heart of God in the Lord Jesus. If we want to know who God is, we should look at Jesus in the Scriptures, because he is the image or clear and perfect picture of who God is.

Verse 15 also tells us that Jesus is "the firstborn over all creation." In biblical times the firstborn son in a family enjoyed a very special place. He also had a unique responsibility: he would inherit the estate or kingdom of the father and be the leader of the family. As the firstborn, he was to be honored and respected in a distinctive way. Jesus enjoys this preeminent position over all creation. The Father placed all things under his control. Jesus is the supreme Son and eternal God and as such is the ruler over all and deserving of respect and dignity. He is the head of the new spiritual family that God the Father is establishing on the earth. This is a family of forgiven and redeemed individuals who have become sons and daughters of his Father.

Notice in verse 16 that all things were created by Jesus and for him. Jesus was not created but is the Creator. Paul tells us that everything in heaven and earth was brought into existence by Christ and for Christ. The earth and all it contains, both visible and invisible, are his. The visible mountains and the invisible winds are his and created by him. All the angelic powers have been created by him and will ultimately bring him glory. All human rulers and kingdoms have served his purposes. They will all bow the knee before him and recognize him as Lord of all on the day of judgment.

Paul reiterated in verse 17 that the Lord Jesus was before all things; he existed before everything we see on this earth. He is the eternal God who is worthy of all our praise and adoration. Jesus holds the world together and gives life and breath to all of his creation.

In verse 18 Paul told the Colossians that this same Jesus is the head of the church, the body of believers. The true church consists of those who have been redeemed from the kingdom of darkness and forgiven of all their sins. Jesus is their sovereign ruler.

Paul went on to say that Jesus "is the beginning." We have already seen this as it refers to the creation of the world. He is also the beginning of the spiritual creation that God is setting apart for himself. Through his death on the cross, the Lord Jesus created a church, a new kingdom of priests for himself. His death opened the door for us to be spiritually reborn into his family. Jesus is the origin of this new creation as well.

Jesus is also "the firstborn from among the dead." He rose from the dead, conquering death which could not hold him. Jesus broke death's hold on humanity. This gives us hope as believers. Through him we too can conquer death. Our hope of victory lies in the Lord.

In everything he deserves to have supremacy. In other words, he deserves to be given the first place in all things. He is worthy of all our praise and adoration. He is our Creator and the one who keeps us day by day. He is our Savior and Head. Without him, we would have nothing. Without him, we would not exist. We owe everything to him.

In verse 19 Paul told the Colossians that God was pleased to have all his fullness dwell in Christ. That is to say, all that God the Father is, the Son is also. Jesus has the full power and authority of God in him. He is God in every sense of the word. To honor the Son is to honor the Father as well. The Son is as deserving of praise and worship as the Father. To dishonor the Son is to dishonor the Father. The Son is completely and fully God.

Through the Son the Father chose to reconcile all things to himself, whether things on earth or things in heaven (verse 20). He did this by making peace through the blood of his Son shed on the cross. There are a couple of things we need to see here.

Notice the desire of the Father and the Son. It was their desire to reconcile all things to themselves. In particular, Paul tells us that God reconciled both things on earth and things in heaven. Sin brought a division between God and his creation. God could have let this world go. He could have chosen to allow us to perish in our sin and rebellion. He did not want to do this, however. He wanted to restore us to a relationship with him. This is the heart of God. Maybe you feel unworthy of this attention and love. Maybe you have lived in sin and rebellion and you don't think that God could really forgive you. Notice here that the desire of the creator, sustainer, and ruler of the world is to reach out to us in love, breaking all barriers to fellowship between sinful people on earth and a holy God in heaven. His great desire is to restore us to fellowship with him. You may not understand this, but don't let it keep you from receiving what he wants to offer. God truly does want you for himself. He willingly sent his Son to live and die so that you could be rescued from the dark kingdom of sin. Don't turn him away.

The second thing we need to see here is that Paul tells us that it is the desire of God to reconcile all things to himself. The fact of the matter is that all of creation suffered the effects of sin. From the day sin entered the world, this whole earth has been groaning under its curse. Adam had to work hard to produce a crop for his family. Things decay and grow old. Disease and sickness have ravaged the earth. Plagues and tragedies have become commonplace. All of creation suffers from sin.

When Paul tells us that it is the desire of God to reconcile all things, he includes the whole creation in this. It is the heart of God to restore blessing to the earth as well as to his children. We see evidence of this in the Old Testament. When God's people turned their backs on him, their crops suffered for it. The blessing of God was removed not only from the lives of his children but also from the land. We see a clear example of this in the book of Hosea: "Hear the word of the LORD, you Israelites, because the LORD has a charge to bring against you who live in the land: 'There is no faithfulness, no love, no acknowledgment of God in the land. There is only cursing, lying and murder, stealing and adultery; they break all bounds, and bloodshed follows bloodshed. Because of this the land mourns, and all who live in it waste away; the beasts of the field and the birds of the air and the fish of the sea are dying'" (Hosea 4:1–3). There was a clear connection between disobedience and the number of fish in the sea. The fish were dying in the sea because of unfaithfulness in the land.

When we turn to God with all our heart, things happen not only in our lives but in our land as well. Listen to words of 2 Chronicles 7:13–14: "When I shut up the heavens so that there is no rain, or command locusts to devour the land or send a plague among my people, if my people, who are called by my name, will humble themselves and pray and seek my face and turn from their wicked ways, then will I hear from heaven and will forgive their sin and will heal their land." The land was suffering because of the people's sin. The writer of 2 Chronicles tells us that if God's people would have humbled themselves and turned from their sin, then God would have not only healed them but their land as well.

We see from this that it is the desire of God to reconcile not only us but the creation as well. He wants to restore all of creation back to its original condition. He created this earth to be a source of blessing to us. Through sin it has become a curse. God's desire is to reverse this curse. Satan and sin have stripped us of the blessing of God. Sin has stripped this earth of his blessing as well. God wants to extend his blessing through Christ to every place that this curse is found. The power of Christ's forgiveness can restore all that the curse of sin has taken from us.

For Consideration:

- What blessings have we received from Christ, according to this passage?

- What does Paul mean when he tells us that Jesus is the firstborn?

- What is God's heart for his creation?

- Why is it so hard for people to open their hearts to what the Lord Jesus wants to do in them?

- What was it like to be under the control and domination of darkness? What difference has it made in your life to be part of the kingdom of his beloved Son?

For Prayer:

- Thank the Lord Jesus for what he has done in rescuing you from the dominion of darkness.

- If you don't know that you are rescued from this dominion of darkness, ask the Lord to set you free today.

- What particular blessing have you received in Christ? Take a moment to thank the Lord for this blessing.

- If you have friends or loved ones who are still under the dominion of darkness, ask the Lord to set them free.

14

Presented Perfect in His Sight

Read Colossians 1:21–29

Paul told the Colossians that it is the desire of the Father to reconcile all things to himself through the cross of his Son. There were individuals in Colosse who had been reconciled to God through the message of the gospel. These individuals accepted the work of the Lord Jesus and were restored to a right relationship with the Father. Paul wanted the Colossians to know that salvation was only the beginning. Since they were saved from the wrath of God, they needed to grow in this relationship with him. Paul told the Colossians that it was his ministry to prepare the body of Christ to meet the Lord. He wanted to present the Colossians to the Lord in a perfect and holy condition.

Paul reminded the Colossians of their condition before they came to know the Lord. They were separated from God and enemies in their minds. At one time they wanted nothing to do with God. All that God stood for, they stood against. God stood for purity; they lived in sin. God stood for morality; they lived in immorality. God was the farthest thing from their minds. Beyond this, however, as his enemies they were destined for judgment. They were headed for an eternal separation from God in hell. They were under his wrath and would suffer the consequences of his anger against them for their sin and rebellion.

While at one time they were enemies to God, the Colossian believers had been reconciled to him through the cross. They deserved God's wrath, but Jesus died for them and took their penalty on himself. He paid the price for them. By accepting the work of Christ, these Colossians were released from the penalty of sin. The barrier between them and God was removed and their relationship restored.

Notice here that while they had been reconciled to God by Christ's payment of their penalty, they were not yet perfect. Paul told the Colossians in verse 22 that God reconciled them through Christ to present them holy in his sight, free from blemish and accusation. The word *to* here could also be translated "in order to." Paul was saying that the Colossians were united to Christ for a purpose. That purpose was so that they could be set free from sin, without character flaws or providing occasion for criticism. Salvation was only the beginning of what God wanted to do in their lives. Since the major obstacle of sin had been overcome and they were right with God, the way was paved for them to draw nearer to God. Until the matter of sin had been dealt with, there could have been no drawing near. Jesus opened the way for all who would accept his death on their behalf to draw near to the Father. He opened the way for sinners to be holy and blameless. This is possible only because Jesus took upon himself the penalty for sin.

As believers, we know that there are still things we need to deal with in our lives. Scripture challenges us to wage war against sin and the flesh. While the penalty for sin is paid, this does not mean that we never fall into sin. The Lord calls us to die to our old, evil nature and live for him (Romans 8:13). This is an ongoing process in our spiritual lives. The death of the Lord Jesus opened the way for us to draw near to God and become more like Christ. This is why we have been saved. We are saved so we can enter into a deeper relationship with the Lord Jesus. We are saved so that we can live in victory over sin.

Paul made it clear to the Colossians that this matter of dealing with the flesh and its evil desires would not be without effort on their part. He told them in verse 23 that the only way they could be holy and without blemish or accusation before God was for them to continue in their faith, established and unmoved from the hope offered in the gospel. This hope is the message of the Lord Jesus coming to rescue a rebellious people from their sin. It is the message of complete forgiveness of sin because of the death of the Lord Jesus on the cross. As believers, we must not lose sight of this hope. We must never let the world or the flesh keep us from living in the reality of our forgiveness in Christ. We must understand that the Lord Jesus came to deal with this matter of sin so that we could be overcomers. We must stand firm in this hope and purpose. This will mean turning from evil. It will mean seeking the Lord with all our heart and striving toward holiness, no matter the cost.

Continuing in the faith involves struggle. God never promised that the Christian journey would be easy. Some have faced tremendous opposition and even death. We must be willing to die to our interests and desires and put the Lord first in our lives. We will be holy, blameless, and without accusation only if we continue in this hope of salvation. Even believers, who have been reconciled to God through the work of the Lord Jesus, still have areas of their lives that have not been completely surrendered to God. Maybe you have accepted the sacrifice of the Lord Jesus and have become his child, but are you striving for holiness? Paul's challenge to the Colossians and to all of us believers is to make it our goal to be flawless in character and above criticism.

Paul saw himself as a servant of the gospel (verse 23). He had committed his life to preaching this gospel and helping people to live in the reality of this hope. Paul felt it was his duty not only to point people to the salvation that was offered them in Christ but also to help them to mature in that salvation. Evangelism and discipleship walk hand in hand. We don't give birth to a baby and walk away from it. We nurture, feed, and care for that baby until it grows into maturity. This is what Paul felt about his work with the Colossians. He saw it as his responsibility not only to see them enter the kingdom of God but also to be presented to Christ as holy and blameless children.

Verse 24 can be somewhat difficult to understand. Paul told the Colossians that he rejoiced to suffer for them and to fill up what was lacking in Christ's suffering. How are we to understand this? We need to see that Paul had no intention of diminishing the finished work of Christ on the cross. By his suffering on the cross, the Lord Jesus accomplished everything that needed to be accomplished for our salvation. He bore all the suffering he needed to bear for our complete and full redemption. Paul was saying here that he was experiencing the persecution and affliction intended for Christ. Paul was addressing the suffering that believers must bear as they seek to live for Christ and expand his kingdom in a hostile world. Paul reminds us in 2 Corinthians that the sufferings of Christ overflow into our lives: "For just as the sufferings of Christ flow over into our lives, so also through Christ our comfort overflows" (2 Corinthians 1:5). And today the enemies of Christ are still inflicting pain on his followers. As his children, we are part of his church, his body on earth. In a physical sense, when our hand feels pain, our whole body suffers. Similarly, when we suffer, the Lord

Jesus also suffers. He grieves with us and goes through our suffering and persecution with us. In this sense, his suffering is not yet finished, although redemption is complete. One day all pain and suffering will be over, and we will be with him forever.

In verse 25 Paul reminded the Colossians that he had been commissioned by God to present the word of God in its fullness. This word had been hidden for ages but now had been revealed to the saints, both Gentile and Jew. What was that word that had been hidden? Paul tells us that it was "Christ in you" (verse 26). We need to examine this and see its connection to the context.

From the beginning of time, there has been a common problem that every human being who walked on this earth has had to face. That problem is sin and how it separates us from God. Because of this problem, humanity has been destined to an eternity of separation from God. In the Garden of Eden God promised that he would break the control of sin. In the generations that followed, man wondered when and how this would take place. How could sinful people and a holy God ever be united? This was a great mystery. The Savior and the plan of salvation were hidden from many generations of people. Paul reminded the Colossians, however, that through the Lord Jesus that plan had been revealed.

God was going to place the Spirit of his Son in the lives and hearts of his people. By this means, he would not only forgive them of their sins but also enable them to be formed into his image. His Son in them would give them a hope of glory in the presence of the Father. The Lord Jesus alone was the guarantee that they would one day be presented as holy people to the Father, spotless and blameless. By his work on the cross and by his constant indwelling in the hearts and lives of believers, Christ would accomplish in them the plan and purpose of the Father.

What a privilege we have in these days! We have seen

the unfolding of God's plan. We have met the Savior. We have experienced the reality of his Holy Spirit living in us. We know in our hearts the wonderful hope of glory in the presence of the Father. It is for us to share this wonderful hope with others. In verse 28 Paul reminded the Colossians that he proclaimed this mystery by admonishing and teaching.

To admonish means to warn or to caution. Paul admonished his listeners concerning this message of Christ in them. Maybe we need to hear the warning of this message again in our day. There are serious implications to this message of Christ in us. If the Spirit of God is in us, we dare not grieve him. If we understand that the Spirit of Christ is in us, we will be careful of what we say, where we go, and what we do. With the Spirit of Christ in us, we are a special people. We have a testimony to keep before the world. We are representatives of the Lord Jesus. Our bodies are the dwelling place of the Holy Spirit. This ought to change how we live and how we do things. Paul's heart was to see believers mature and become everything they needed to be in Christ.

There is another aspect to this warning as well. How many times have people tried to live the Christian life on their own? They believe that good works are enough to merit a place in the kingdom of God. This message of "Christ in you" reminds us that there is no other way for us to be saved. Christ alone is our salvation. He alone can bring reconciliation between us and God. Paul warned of the futility of trusting in human effort for salvation. He reminded his readers that the only hope of glory they had was the presence of the Spirit of Christ in them.

Paul taught this truth everywhere he went. As we have already seen, there are many implications to this truth about Christ living in us. This truth ought to change our lives and our ways. Paul's desire was to teach Christians how to live after they had the presence of Christ in them. Notice that the reason Paul admonished and taught this truth was so that those who heard it could be perfected in their character (see verse 28). If you want to become mature and like Christ, you need to understand this message of "Christ in you." You need to stop trying to live the Christian life on your own and instead let the Spirit of God be your guide and strength. He alone can perfect you.

Paul's great heart cry was to see believers grow to perfect maturity. Notice in verse 29 that he labored and struggled with all his energy to do this. Those who are involved in this ministry of perfecting believers realize how difficult a task this is. Praise the Lord for those who minister in this way. To this end, God has raised up pastors, teachers, and evangelists. They minister through visiting, listening, counseling, and exhorting believers. They spend long hours and sleepless nights concerned for the body of Christ. They pray, they preach, and they weep. They do this because, like Paul, their greatest joy is to see believers moving on to perfection.

There is one more very important detail we need to see in verse 29. Notice that Paul labored and struggled not with his own energy but with the energy that was given to him by the Spirit of Christ, who dwelt in him. How easy it would be for us to miss this point. Paul's boundless energy was not his own. He attributed his energy to the powerful work of the Spirit of God in his life. What a difference it makes when we let the Spirit of God guide and lead us in all things. The ministry of perfecting the saints is the ministry of the Holy Spirit. If we are open, the Spirit of Christ will lead us and motivate us. He will strengthen and equip us in this task. How much we need him to work through us!

We see in this passage that God has reached out to us to save us and to perfect us in Christ. Through the Lord Jesus the door has been opened for the Spirit to minister in us and through us. Paul's great desire was to see those finish well who had begun their life with Christ. Paul wanted to see them stand before Christ on that final day, unashamed, spotless, and holy. To this end he labored and struggled. To this end we too must labor. May God give us a heart like Paul's. May he raise up in our day a people whose heart cry is to draw near to Christ.

For Consideration:

- Why has God saved us from sin? Is salvation the end or the beginning? Explain.

- What do we learn here about the importance of Christ in us? Why is it important that we understand this message of Christ in us?

- How do you know that Christ is in you? What are the evidences?

- In this passage what is the heart of Paul for believers?

For Prayer:

- Thank the Lord for putting his Holy Spirit in your life.

- What needs to be perfected in you? Ask the Lord to break what needs to be broken and heal what needs to be healed.

- Ask the Lord to show you how you can be an instrument in his hands to help in the perfecting of the saints.

15

The Riches of a Complete Understanding

Read Colossians 2:1–7

I f there is one thing we learn about the apostle Paul, it is that he had a tremendous burden on his heart for the maturity and growth of believers. In the last meditation, the apostle told us that his great concern was to present the Colossians pure and blameless to Christ. Paul was driven by a passion to see believers grow in the Lord and become everything God intended them to be.

As we begin chapter 2 of Colossians, we continue to see Paul's passion for the Colossians and their growth in Christ. He told them that he wanted them to know how much he was struggling for them and the believers in the region of Laodicea. Paul had never met many of these individuals, but he still struggled in his heart for them.

I find it interesting to see how Paul struggled in his own soul and mind. There is a time for us to rest, and there is a time for us to earnestly toil. There are those who say that there ought never to be a struggle in the Christian life.

Anyone who has passion for advancing God's kingdom will also know contention. There are times when we need to simply place our burdens on the Lord and learn to rest in his provision and guidance, and there are times when we need to struggle. We need to remember that we are in a war between good and evil (Ephesians 6:12). If we are concerned about the kingdom of God, we will feel pain and agony when the glory of the Lord is at stake. We will feel grief for those who are lost in sin. We will ache for those who are hurting and wrestling with strongholds of sin in their lives. We will cry out to God for the expansion of his kingdom in the lives and hearts of men and women.

Paul was a man of passion for the kingdom of God, and it was this passion that caused his deep struggle and desire to work tirelessly for God's glory. We all need to have this sort of passion. What causes you struggle in your ministry? What breaks your heart? What is your particular passion for the kingdom? There are times when the Lord will not give us rest. He does this so that we will be driven to minister. That struggle will keep us from becoming comfortable, careless, and lazy in our spiritual lives.

Paul told the Colossians in verse 2 the nature of his struggle. His heart was burdened to see the Colossians and the Laodiceans encouraged in heart and united in love so that they would have the full riches of a complete understanding of their position in Christ. We need to examine what Paul was saying here.

Paul's desire was that these people would be encouraged and unified in the love of Christ. We can assume that these individuals already knew the Lord Jesus as their Savior. They were part of the kingdom of God. Despite the fact that they were children of God, they still needed encouragement. Even believers can be blinded to the reality of what they have in the Lord Jesus. The cares and concerns of this world can hide from our eyes the beauty of Christ and our relationship with him. The burden of care and responsibility can weigh us down. Ministry can overwhelm us. We need to be reassured and refreshed in our relationship with Christ and see his love and care in a new way.

Paul also wanted to see these believers united in love. It comes as no surprise that believers have different personalities and priorities. We do not always see things in the same way. This can lead to division in the body of Christ. These divisions can blind us to the reality of Christ and his feelings toward us. By reaching out in love, we demonstrate to our brothers and sisters the love of Christ for them. When we understand how much the Lord loves his children, we will be far less willing to speak evil of them. Paul wanted to see the body of Christ united in their love for each other. This was part of moving on to perfection.

Notice that Paul wanted the believers to be encouraged and united in love "so that they may have the full riches of complete understanding" (verse 2). There is a clear connection between their encouragement and unity in love and their understanding of their riches in Christ. We need to see this connection.

Disunity in the body will blind us to the fullness of our riches in Christ. Very often the Lord will use his people to be the vehicles of his love. When the Lord wants to encourage us, he will often do so by sending a brother or sister. When he wants to provide for our needs, he will ask someone who has what we need to share it with us, just at the right time. He will use godly men and women to counsel us when we need guidance and direction. What happens, however, when the body refuses to listen to the Lord in this manner? How much more difficult it is for us to see the fullness of our riches in Christ when we see all around us believers arguing and protecting their own interests! We see the fullness of our riches in Christ as the body ministers in his name to one another. The world also sees the fullness of Christ in how we minister to each other.

Paul prayed that the Colossians and Laodiceans would be encouraged and united in love so that they would have the riches of a complete understanding of what they had in Christ. Notice, however, that understanding what they had in Christ was not the end. Paul wanted them to have the riches of a full understanding in order that they might know Christ, the mystery of God revealed to them. You can know what you have in Christ without really knowing Christ. You can speak about the peace and joy that come from the Lord Jesus and still not experience them in reality. You can quote all the verses in the Bible about God providing for your every need, but have you lived in this reality? There are many Christians who know their riches intellectually but are not living in the reality of those riches every day. They look and live like their unbelieving neighbors. Intellectual knowledge is not enough. We need to know Christ and experience him. Theology must also be accompanied by experience.

Paul reminds us in verse 3 that in Jesus are hidden all the treasures of wisdom and knowledge. We have already seen that the universe was created by the Lord Jesus. For centuries we have studied this universe and have not yet fathomed the depths of it. The wisdom of the Lord Jesus in the creation of this universe has baffled the greatest human minds. Beyond all this, however, God is unfolding his spiritual purposes for this universe through the Lord Jesus. God is creating a people for himself. The Lord Jesus is the center of that purpose. Without his work we would never have been united with the Father. He defeated death and the grave. He overcame Satan and sin. He created and sustains the universe, and we owe every breath we breathe to him. He is the source of all our ability to think, work, and speak. All the treasures of wisdom are in him. He knows all things. Nothing would exist without him.

Paul taught these things so that the Colossians would not be deceived by the arguments of those among them who taught error. These individuals had carefully reasoned arguments that sounded very intelligent but were contrary to what they had learned from Christ. Paul was asking the Colossians to consider for a moment that Christ is the source of all wisdom. No matter how skilled these false teachers were, there were things they simply did not understand. Will you believe the one through whom the purpose of God the Father is unfolding, or will you believe sinful humans whose understanding is limited? The answer should be obvious. The arguments of the false teachers were carefully reasoned but contrary to God. We must listen to God and him alone. Paul feared that the church in Colosse would be deceived by these skillful but false teachers. Paul was concerned about these believers, and even though he could not physically be with them, he was with them in spirit (verse 5). His heart and his prayers went out to them. It delighted him that they were being faithful. He prayed that they would continue to be faithful and not be deceived by those false prophets and teachers who came into their midst.

To be mature in Christ means not only knowing the truth he teaches but also living faithfully in that truth. In verse 6 Paul challenged the Colossians to walk in Christ just as they had received him. In this context Paul was speaking about the false teachers who had come to Colosse. These deceptive teachers had well-reasoned arguments, but they taught a counterfeit gospel. They were promoting a lifestyle that was contrary to the principles Christ had taught them. Paul told the Colossians that they were to live in Christ just as they had received him. How had they received Christ? They had received him by faith. Christ did not come to them because they deserved it or merited it. They simply heard his voice and obeyed. They opened their hearts to receive what he wanted to give.

This is how God calls us to live today. Just as receiving Christ was not by our own efforts, neither is our life in him. There are those who teach that to be a Christian you need to *do* this or that. They have reduced the Christian life down to a set of rules and regulations. This is not what the Christian life is about. It is about opening up our hearts to what God wants to do. It is about listening and hearing God. It is about knowing him. You can no more live the Christian life in your own efforts than you can save yourself. When we came to the Lord Jesus, we had to say, "Lord, I cannot save myself; you must come and do the saving." This is how we need to live our lives too. We need to come to the Lord Jesus and say, "Lord, I cannot live this life you have required; you are going to have to do it." Having said this, we then need to listen and obey. We need to let him work through us. We are the glove and he is the hand that moves the glove.

Many times I have failed to understand this principle. I somehow have believed that I could live the Christian life by myself. I knew that the Holy Spirit was given, but I felt that it was only to help me where I failed. I did not realize that unless the Spirit of God did the work, it was to no avail. Paul spoke of the power of God moving him. It was as if Paul could not help but minister. The Spirit of God was driving him and telling him what to do and say. Paul was the instrument, but God was doing the work.

What a blessing it is to experience God in this way. We are carried along by his Spirit. You can't save yourself nor can you truly live the Christian life as God requires by yourself. Let God do it. Open your heart to him, as a vessel to be used. Let him work, minister, and lead. You will be surprised at what he will do. In so doing, you will be strengthened in your faith. You will have much cause to be thankful to him. You will overflow with thankfulness for the opportunity to be an instrument in his hands. What an incredible thing it is to be an instrument of God! What an incredible thing it is to be saved from our sins and have the hope of eternal life in the presence of God! We are indeed a very rich people. The enemy wants to take our eyes off what we have in the Lord. The enemy does not want us to understand our privilege in Christ. Paul's prayer was that the Colossians would never lose sight of their position and riches of being in Christ.

For Consideration:

• What riches do you have in Christ?

• What is your particular passion in ministry? What has God called you to struggle with in ministry?

• What is the difference between knowing the riches we have in Christ and experiencing them in reality?

• What did Paul mean when he told the Colossians that they were to live as they had received Christ? Is this how you have been living and ministering?

For Prayer:

• Thank the Lord for the way he has blessed you in abundance.

• Ask the Lord to open your heart to be an instrument in his hands. Ask him to help you get out of the way and let him work through you.

• Have you found yourself losing sight of the Lord Jesus in your situation or ministry? Ask him to renew your understanding of his presence.

16

Christ versus Human Traditions

Read Colossians 2:8–23

F rom the context of this book, we understand that certain individuals had come to Colosse with a teaching that was contrary to what Paul had taught. They were promoting the need to follow a set of traditions and laws in order to be saved. Paul took a firm stand against these individuals in this chapter.

In verse 8 Paul began by telling the Colossians that they were to be very careful to see that no one took them captive by means of hollow and deceptive philosophy. Philosophy is a human attempt to make sense of the universe. Notice what Paul has to say about this philosophy: it depended on human traditions and the basic principles of this world, but it did not depend on Christ. The philosophy that Paul spoke about was a human attempt to analyze the world and to try to make sense of it. Those who promoted this kind of philosophy did not turn to the Scriptures or to Christ for answers. They turned instead to their own reasoning. They were very logical and skillful in their presentation, but they were wrong. Paul did not want the Colossians to be deceived by these false teachers and their philosophy.

Any attempt to understand the meaning of this life apart from Christ will always fail. Only in him does life make sense. In this context Paul reminded the Colossians in verse 9 that the fullness of deity lived in the human body of Jesus. In other words, Jesus Christ is God and the creator of the universe and everything in it. Therefore, he would know the purpose of life. According to Paul, understanding life required a turning to Christ the Creator and Savior. Any effort to understand life apart from Christ was deceptive, immature, and futile.

From this starting point, Paul moved on to tell the Colossians something about their position in Christ and the purpose for which he had created them. Paul began in verse 10 by reminding them that they had been given complete sufficiency for every need in Christ, who is the head over every power or authority. There is no power or wisdom superior to Christ. He is the Lord of all lords and the King of all kings. Paul was telling the Colossians that they had the privilege as believers of being filled with Christ, who is the sole source of spiritual maturity. They did not need to look to the world for their wisdom.

Second, in verse 11 Paul reminded the Colossians that in Christ they were circumcised by the putting off of the sinful nature. This circumcision was not a physical circumcision but a spiritual one. In other words, when they came to the Lord Jesus, he cut off their attachment to the sinful nature. They were given new hearts and minds. For the first time, they were able to understand the purpose and plan of God. The attraction to sinful desires was broken. The Spirit of God changed their hearts and ways of thinking. The old nature was cut off (circumcised). They were a new people whose thoughts were transformed. They no longer depended on futile human philosophies but were connected to the source of all wisdom.

Paul went on to tell the Colossians in verse 12 that they had been buried with Christ in baptism and raised with him through faith in the power of God. Paul told them first that they were baptized with Christ. This baptism was Christ's death. Jesus spoke of this in the Gospel of Luke: "But I have a baptism to undergo, and how distressed I am until it is completed!" (Luke 12:50). When the Lord Jesus spoke these words, he had already been baptized by John, so he was speaking of another baptism. It is obvious from the context of Luke 12 that the reason why Jesus was so distressed about this baptism was because the baptism of which he spoke was his death.

Paul also spoke about death as a baptism in Romans: "Or don't you know that all of us who were baptized into Christ Jesus were baptized into his death?" (Romans 6:3). When Paul told the Colossians that they were buried with Christ in his baptism, he was telling them that when the Lord Jesus went through his baptism of death on the cross, they died with him in a spiritual sense. He was lifted up on that cross because of our sin. It was our punishment that he took on the cross. He did not die for himself but for us. God looked down from heaven and saw our sins on the shoulders of his Son. The Father turned his face from his Son and punished him with holy wrath, the penalty for sin. We were spiritually put to death on that cross with Christ as he bore our penalty. It was as if we ourselves were put on that cross and died.

Paul went on to say that just as we died with Christ, we were also raised with him (verse 12). When the dead body of Jesus was put in the grave, our old sin nature was buried also. When the Father raised Jesus from the grave with a glorified body, he raised us up also to live victoriously. The fact that God raised Christ from the dead is the sign that God accepted the price Christ paid. God was proclaiming that the power of sin is broken. The penalty is paid. We have hope.

In verse 12 Paul continued to explain that once we were dead in our sins and living in the uncircumcision of our sinful nature. That is to say, before the sinful nature was cut off, we were still living under its control. Jesus took our sin with him to the cross. Having conquered sin and paid the penalty, forgiveness could then be granted to all who would accept Christ's payment on their behalf. Now because of Christ, there is complete forgiveness of sin.

Jesus died for sins—past, present, and future. This has a very important application. If all my sins have been paid for, then there is nothing more I can do to merit salvation. Everything has been done. Paul told the Colossians in verse 14 that Christ's death canceled the written code (the law) with all its regulations. Jesus fulfilled the law, and then God took the law and nailed it to the cross with Jesus (verse 14). This means that no one can be saved by means of the law. Jesus is the way of salvation. Any sin that we commit now is covered by the cross. When it comes to salvation, the law has no value. To think that we can somehow get to heaven by observing the law and doing good works is to fail to understand what the Lord Jesus did on the cross for us. Paul is trying to communicate the foolishness of the false teaching of the day that stressed salvation by following a set of teachings and regulations.

Not only did Jesus deal with the question of sin on the cross but he also disarmed powers and authorities (verse 15). Who are these powers and authorities? On the one hand, they may be those earthly powers with all their worldly philosophies. This world has its ideas of the meaning of life, but all of these philosophies are empty. Jesus showed us the way to live. Those who find him find true meaning in life. By his death on the cross, the Lord Jesus showed the world the foolishness of these worldly philosophies.

Beyond this, however, Jesus also disarmed spiritual powers and authorities. When the Lord Jesus died on the cross, he broke the power of Satan. Spiritual forces lifted the Lord up on that cross, mocking him and spitting on him, but Jesus overcame them. He broke their power. Now, at the name of Jesus, Satan and his angels flee. They have been defeated. Their destiny is sealed. They have no more ultimate power over those who are in Christ. Evil forces may oppress and cause believers great problems and difficulties in this life, but these forces will ultimately fail. They have been disarmed. The cross broke the power of Satan and his angels to halt God's redemptive plans.

The penalty of sin has been paid and Satan has been disarmed. Christ has done it all. Paul told the Colossians, therefore, that in light of these facts, they should never let anyone judge them on the basis of what they eat and drink or whether they celebrate a certain religious festival or practice the Sabbath. In other words, their salvation had nothing to do with whether they practiced the Sabbath. It had nothing to do with whether they practiced the food laws of the Old Testament. Paul was clear here. If our salvation is accomplished completely by Jesus on the cross, we cannot judge whether other individuals are in a right relationship with Christ on the basis of the law. All that matters is whether they have accepted the Lord Jesus and the payment he has made for them on the cross.

The law had provided ancient Israel with God's holy standard for righteousness. It had showed the Israelites that they were sinners, who could not keep God's requirements. The law and all its obligations were graciously given to prepare the hearts of God's people for the coming of their Christ, who would accomplish what they were not able to accomplish in their own efforts through the law. The law was intended to reveal sin and also provide a sacrificial system through which sinners could relate to a holy God.

Christ fulfilled both these aspects of the law. His perfect life reveals our sin and his death provides a way for us to relate to a holy God. Christ replaced the law with himself. Faith in Christ alone is the only way of salvation.

It is in this light that Paul told the Colossians that they were not to let anyone disqualify them for the prize. The false teachers were preaching another gospel. They were instructing believers to worship angels. These teachers claimed to have great visions and dreams. They went into great detail describing these wonderful images (verse 18). They tried to look spiritual, but they were worldly. They had all kinds of ideas and directions to give those who listened to them, but they were in reality pointing others away from the Lord Jesus and what he had done. Paul reminded the Colossians in verse 19 that these false teachers had "lost connection with the Head" (the Lord Jesus).

Paul used the illustration of the human body. Christ is the head and believers are the body. Just as the body cannot function without the head, so believers need to be connected with Christ. The moment we let our eyes stray from the Lord Jesus, we lose sight of everything that is important. We find ourselves on a track that will lead us astray.

Paul encouraged the Colossians in verse 20 to remember that they had died with Christ to the philosophies and principles of this world. Because of this, they were not to return to these things again. There were believers who were living as though their salvation depended on keeping the law. The lives of these individuals consisted of following a set of rules and regulations: "Do not handle! Do not taste! Do not touch!" (verse 21).

The false teachers preached law and traditions. Their emphasis was not on the Lord Jesus but rather on all the do's and don'ts of the law. They judged the spirituality of individuals by whether they kept certain rules. Paul told the Colossians that these rules were based on human commands and teachings and not on Christ. These regulations had an appearance of wisdom but were not from God. Those who lived by these traditions actually worshiped themselves. Like the Pharisees, they took pride in the lie that they did all that was required of them. They presented themselves to others as being disciplined and spiritual people willing to sacrifice everything. They treated their bodies harshly and sacrificed much. Maybe they fasted and denied themselves the pleasures of this world. But all these practices really had no value in changing their hearts toward God. They were no closer to God after following all their traditions. If anything, they were farther from him because they denied their real need of Christ and his work.

Paul was not teaching that we can live the way we please. He was saying, however, that the law will never save us. Paul understood that when we get our eyes off the Lord and his work, we lose sight of all that matters. Our hope must be rooted solidly in the Lord Jesus alone. Rules and regulations will never save us. Jesus has done it all.

In this section we see how Paul challenged the Colossians to beware of those who taught another gospel. Paul focused attention on the Lord Jesus, his life and death. Paul challenged his readers to reject any teaching that did not emphasize the work of Christ alone for salvation and holy living. Everything was to begin and end with Christ.

For Consideration:

• What meaning does life have without Christ? Explain. Why is it important that we seek meaning in Him?

• What does Paul tell us Jesus has done for us on the cross?

- If Jesus died for our sins—past, present, and future—all our sins are covered. How does this show us that the law can never save us?

- What kind of things can distract us from focusing on Christ and his work alone for our salvation?

- What is the difference between trusting the law and trusting Christ?

- Does trusting Christ alone for our salvation mean that we no longer have to be concerned about how we live? Explain.

For Prayer:

- Thank the Lord for covering all your sins on the cross.

- Ask the Lord to teach you more fully what Christ's death means for you.

- Thank the Lord that we do not have to merit our salvation.

- Ask the Lord to fill you even more by his Holy Spirit so you will be increasingly motivated to serve from a heart of love.

17

Putting to Death the Evil Nature

Read Colossians 3:1–10

I n the last chapter, the apostle Paul spoke to the Colossians about the work of the Lord Jesus on the cross. He reminded them that when the Lord Jesus died on that cross, he took their sins with him. His death paid their penalty. When he rose from the dead, they directly benefited. His resurrection assured them of victory over sin and death. Jesus rose not just for himself but for us as well. If we died with him on that cross, we also rose with him from the grave. Christ acted on our behalf when he died and when he rose. This being the case, there is a very clear application for us.

Paul told the Colossians in verse 1 that because they were raised with Christ, they were to set their minds on things above, where Christ was seated. They were no longer to set their minds on the things of this earth. This does not mean that we cannot enjoy the good things of this earth. What it does mean, however, is that the things of this earth should never be our central focus. God has given us many wonderful things to enjoy. The world that we live in is a gift from our Creator for our benefit. There are those, however, whose focus is entirely on the things of this earth. This world begins to mean more to them than the things of God. They become attracted by the pleasures and possessions of this world and set their minds on these. God gets pushed aside. Paul told the Colossians that because of what the Lord Jesus had done for them, they were to set their minds on the things of God.

Jesus came to set us free from the futile pursuit of worldly goods. All these things will perish in the end. They will have no value in eternity. Someone could have all the possessions of this world and still spend an eternity without Christ. Compared to knowing Christ, all these things mean nothing. Christ, who created us, knows how to fill our hearts with satisfaction and joy. We were created for Christ and the things of this earth will never completely satisfy. Christ came to open the way for us to find the true meaning and purpose of life. He came to open the door for us to enter the presence of the Father, forgiven and cleansed of all our impurities. For this reason, Paul challenges us all to set our minds on heavenly matters. Only in this will we find meaning and purpose.

In verse 3 Paul reminded the Colossians that they died with Christ, who carried their sins on his shoulders when he went to the cross. The cross was not the end but the beginning of something new. Just as a seed is planted in the ground, so we too went with Christ from the cross to the grave. Just as a seed sprouts and produces new life, however, so we too in Christ were given new life. That life is in Christ now. We belong to him. The new life we have is a spiritual life that comes from him as the source. Christ can now live in our hearts by his Holy Spirit. All who have received this new life must learn to live in it. We are to put to death whatever belongs to the earthly nature and live according to the new nature. Maturity in Christ is not an instant event. It is something that comes over time, as we learn to recognize and die to the old sinful nature. While we have been freed from the old nature by Christ, that old nature is still alive in our flesh.

I find the best way to describe what happens in the life of the believer is by using the example of divorce. As sinners, we were married to the flesh. Our allegiance was to the flesh and its way of thinking. When we came to know the Lord Jesus, we divorced that old nature. Legally, when we became a Christian, we changed our allegiance. We divorced the flesh and were married to Christ. The old nature is still around, however, and wants to get back with us. But because we divorced, we now have no more right to that relationship. We must now be faithful to the Lord God and the new nature of his Spirit. It is possible for us to still lust after the ways of the old nature, but we are called to resist that temptation. Instead, we are to set our minds on Christ as our new and perfect companion and partner.

The earthly nature longs to be fed. You don't have to live very long to experience the pull of lust and greed. If we are to be true to the Lord Jesus, we will have to turn away from those things that feed the earthly, sinful nature. If you struggle with sexual lusts, then you will need to keep yourself from those things that will tempt you and feed those evil desires of the flesh. There are places you will need to stay away from and things you need to stop reading or watching. To die to the flesh and the earthly nature is to discipline ourselves to starve that nature. This is a lifelong process. As long as we live in an earthly body, our sin nature will cry out for satisfaction of its lusts. We must make conscious decisions to choose what is right. It is not easy to die to the sinful cries of the flesh. Pulling ourselves away from those things that satisfy that earthly nature will be difficult. To die to sin is to deny it the satisfaction it desires.

Paul reminded the Colossians in verse 6 that the Lord Jesus came to set them free from these evil desires. These desires satisfy the flesh for a moment, but in the end they destroy all those who fall into their trap. The day is coming, said Paul in verse 6, when the wrath of God will be revealed against these things. There is no hope in the ways of the world. The world cannot ultimately satisfy human needs. The Lord himself will judge the earth and those who cling to the ways of this earth. The wise will set their minds on the things of God.

The Colossians used to live to please these evil lusts and desires. But since the Lord Jesus died for them and forgave their sins, they were to turn from these things and live for him. Anger, rage, malice, slander, and filthy language belong to this evil nature. Have you not had times in your life when you lashed out in anger against someone? There is something in our sinful nature that is satisfied by such outbursts. The anger begins to boil in our flesh and in an instant we lash out. In that moment the sinful cravings of the heart are satisfied. By giving way to the flesh, we grieve the Spirit of God in us. Every decision we make in the course of the day will be either a decision to feed the earthly, sinful nature or to please the Spirit of God. No matter how much we grow in the Lord, we will have to deal with this matter.

Instead of feeding that earthly nature, Paul challenged the Colossians to "put on the new self" (verse 10). Instead of releasing that anger and bitterness, they were to put on the robe of forgiveness. Instead of allowing lust to overcome them, they were to put on the robe of purity and praise. Instead of giving in to the earthly nature, they were to turn to the Spirit of God and seek him and his purposes.

Paul reminded the Colossians in verse 10 of how they were being renewed into the image of their Creator. This is an ongoing process in the life of the believer. Daily we ought to be growing more and more in biblical knowledge, without which there can be no spiritual growth.

It is important for us to see that Paul spoke of this dying to the earthly nature in the context of his discussion of the law. Christ took the law with him to the cross. The law has no more benefit when it comes to the question of salvation. All our sins are covered by the blood of Christ. Forgiveness is ours apart from the law. This does not mean, however, that we can live the way we want to live. We are to learn to recognize the earthly nature and die to it. We are to learn to listen to the Spirit of God and live according to his ways. The law told us what to do and what not to do, but it could not enable us to do what was required. The Lord Jesus did what the law could never do. He forgives us from the penalty of our sin and put his Holy Spirit in us to enable us to live in righteousness. Instead of turning to the law, we now turn to the Spirit of God. We no longer trust in our natural ability to obey the law. We trust in the work of the Lord Jesus on the cross. Our trust now is in the Spirit of Christ in us. We realize that in our own efforts we cannot meet the perfect standard that God has set. We trust completely in the Spirit of God to do this work. We trust in him to change our hearts. We trust in him to break our rebellion and hardness of heart. We surrender to him and what he wants to do in us.

Paul's challenge to us here is to deny the flesh its satisfaction. The old nature must be put to death. It was to enable us to do this that Christ came. He died to set us free from the power of sin and death. He died so that the Holy Spirit could come to live in us. We must trust in the ministry of the Holy Spirit in us. We must surrender to him and die to the desires of the earthly nature.

For Consideration:

- Why did the Lord Jesus come to this earth? What does this mean for us and how we are to live today?

- What does it mean to die to the earthly nature?

- How can we recognize the earthly nature?

- What is the difference between trying to live by the law and living by the Spirit?

For Prayer:

- Ask the Lord to show you the areas of your life that you need to die to.

- Thank the Lord that he has given you his Holy Spirit to enable you to live the life he requires.

- Commit yourself to dying to the desires of your earthly nature. Ask God for strength to do this.

18

Life in the Body

Read Colossians 3:11–17

In the last meditation, we saw how Paul challenged the Colossians to die to the earthly nature. They were to do this because Jesus had come to set them free from this world and its sinful desires, which lead to despair and death in the end. While salvation does not depend on obedience to the law, Paul challenged the Colossians, in light of who they were in Christ and what the Lord Jesus had done for them, to live lives that conformed to the image of their Creator. Believers should do this not because the law requires it but simply to please the Lord and live for him. Believers have been freed from their old way of living.

Paul then moved to a discussion about human relationships in the church. He reminded the Colossians that in the body of Christ there are no categories of race or social standing—all believers are one in the Lord. The Jew and the Greek were on equal footing when it came to salvation. It did not matter whether they were circumcised. They could be from an uncivilized barbarian tribe or be a rural, Scythian shepherd and still be part of the family of God. Both the slave and the free were equal before God. In verse 11 Paul told the Colossians that "Christ is in all." We should not see by this that Christ is in every person. What Paul meant was that Christ is in all who trust him for salvation, despite their rank in society or nationality. All who trust Christ can equally know his salvation.

Since the Lord Jesus saves people of all races and social standing, they are all equally our brothers and sisters in the Lord. The Lord expects us, therefore, as a chosen and holy people, to love one another. Paul challenged the Colossians to clothe themselves with compassion (verse 12). They were to feel the pains and struggles of their brothers and sisters and respond in kindness toward them. They were to willingly sacrifice in order to meet the needs of those around them. Kindness was to be their attitude.

This ministry to one another was not to come from pride or selfish ambition. Paul encouraged his readers to act out of humility, gentleness, and patience. As believers in the body of Christ, we will not always see things in the same way. We will have different priorities. As we minister to one another, we will need great patience. In humility we stoop down to serve. We minister with a gentle spirit that blesses and encourages. The only way we can do this is by making ourselves servants like Jesus, who considered the needs of others to be more important than his temporal comfort.

Verse 13 tells us that we are to bear with our brothers and sisters and forgive whatever grievances we have against them. In saying this, Paul recognized the reality of problems in the body of Christ, the church. Troubles will come between believers. What do we do when we are wronged or hurt by another believer? Paul tells us that we need to be patient with one another and forgive.

The word *bear* means "to tolerate or to endure." The

idea is that we are to accept each other even when we don't particularly like the way the other person does things. Sometimes other believers will treat us wrongly. Paul tells us to endure. He tells us that we need to be willing to tolerate the failures of others in the body. Paul was not blind to the fact that the body would have difficulties. Like children in the same family, believers will struggle in their relationships. Instead of tolerating each other, however, we often engage in criticism and ridicule. We need to bear with each other by being gentle, humble, and kind. This is how Christ treats us. He expects us to do no less for our brothers and sisters in Christ.

Paul went on in verse 13 to tell the Colossians that they were to forgive one another. People will hurt us and we will hurt them. In these times we are to remember how the Lord Jesus treated us when we were his enemies. He forgave all our sin. He loved us despite our rebellion. This is how we are to treat those who hurt us. We are to forgive them just as the Lord forgave us. However, there are those who want to hold blame in their hearts. These individuals think that they have a right to be angry and bitter, but this will only destroy their witness and keep them from maturing.

In verse 14 Paul reminded the Colossians that above all else they were to "put on love." Love is the glue that binds all these other virtues together. We cannot truly demonstrate gentleness, humility, patience, and forgiveness if we do not love. The reason we do not forgive is that we do not love as Christ loved us. We have set conditions on our love. We will love as long as the other person treats us in a certain way. The reason we don't show gentleness is because we are lacking in love. If we want to demonstrate the kindness, humility, and patience spoken of in this chapter, we need to get on our knees and ask God to help us love. Other virtues will come easier when we begin with love.

Not only are we to learn to love each other in Christ,

but Paul also tells us to "let the peace of Christ rule" in our hearts. The reason why we are to let this peace rule is that we are all members of the same body and are called to live in peace. There is a connection between letting the peace of Christ rule in our hearts and being at peace with each other. Sometimes it is quite easy to let others upset us. In those times we can turn to the Lord Jesus and commit our way to him. We can look up to him and realize that while this problem seems overwhelming, the Lord is big enough to take care of it. We must remember in these times that the Lord will care for us and do what is right. He can even take the trials we are facing and use them for good in our lives. Only when we look to the Lord in our time of trial can we know this peace. He comforts us and strengthens us. He fills us with his peace so that we are able to live above the problems we are facing. When problems come we can let the flesh respond and seek revenge, or we can wait patiently on the Lord and let his peace reign in our hearts. However, we can only let the peace of Christ rule in our hearts if we are in a right relationship with God. If we have anger in our hearts, we will not be at peace with Christ, and his peace cannot rule in us.

Notice in verse 15 that Paul added something else to his discussion about the relationship of brothers and sisters in Christ. He told the Colossians that they needed to learn how to be thankful. How can we be thankful when things are difficult? How can we be thankful when someone has harmed us or said something against us? The fact of the matter is that if we focus on the things that others have done against us, very likely we will not be thankful. Very often the things we wrestle with in our relationships keep us from seeing any good at all. Maybe it is only one thing that clouds a relationship. This does not mean that everything else is bad. Satan wants us to focus on the negative instead of seeing the positive. Take a moment to consider some positive aspects about a difficult relationship you have with another person and focus on those things. Learn to look for and rejoice in the positive elements, and be thankful that the Lord is in control.

In our relationship with others in the body of Christ, we need to let the word of Christ dwell in us richly. That word will keep us and guide us in the times we are tempted to speak out or act in anger against our brother. Beyond that, however, that word will also convict us of our own sin and draw us closer to the Lord.

As we live together as brothers and sisters in Christ, we are to teach and admonish or warn each other with wisdom. We are to minister to each other and watch out for each other. We cannot mature in Christ on our own. We need the support and encouragement of others in the body of Christ.

Verse 16 makes it clear that this matter of warning and teaching each other can be done in a very creative way. Paul told the Colossians to do this as they sang psalms, hymns, and spiritual songs with gratitude in their hearts to God. If you are involved in a musical ministry, you need to keep this focus. Music is not just for entertainment and worship. It is also for the purpose of teaching and warning the body. God is pleased to take his words put to music and bless, warn, and instruct his people. Each of us has a responsibility to our brothers and sisters in Christ to warn, instruct, and encourage them in the Lord.

Paul concluded his discussion on relationships in the body with a statement about doing everything as unto the Lord. When we speak to a brother or a sister or when we reach out to minister by some deed, we are to do so in the name of the Lord Jesus. If you do something in the name of Jesus, you do it representing him. If you represent him, you must be careful how you act or speak. You must be a good representative. You must speak as he would speak. You must act as he would act. Beyond this, however, we need to realize that whatever we say to fellow believers, we are also saying to Christ, who died for them. If we mistreat them, we will have to answer to Christ.

Paul speaks here about our responsibilities to each other. While he tells us we are no longer under law, he is careful to' remind us that this does not mean that we are a people without principles. God has a standard for us to live by. That standard is not the law but Christ himself. We must look to him, not only for our example but also for our enabling.

For Consideration:

- Are there individuals that you have a hard time accepting? What does Paul tell us about bearing with each other?

- Take a moment to consider a relationship with a person whom you have a hard time accepting. What is in this relationship that you can be thankful for?

- How can we let the peace of Christ rule in our hearts? How does this help us in our relationships with each other?

- What role has God given you in the body of Christ? How do your gifts help the body?

For Prayer:

- Ask the Lord to give you a greater love for those you have difficulty loving.

- Take a moment to thank the Lord for something about a person you have trouble loving.

- Ask the Lord to fill you with his peace so that you can be at peace with those whom you find difficult to love.

19

Relationships in the Body

Read Colossians 3:18–4:1

Paul had been speaking to the Colossians about relationships in the body of Christ in general. In this final section of Chapter 3, Paul challenged the church in some very particular relationships. He gave some practical guidelines for Christian households.

Wives

Paul began with a word to the wives. He challenged them to submit to their husbands. The Greek word used here for *submit* is the word *hupotasso*. This word, when used in a military context, means "to arrange oneself under the command of a superior officer." When used in a nonmilitary context, the word speaks of a voluntary cooperation. The one who submits is one who cooperates with someone else. The one who submits takes on the burden of the person being submitted to. When Paul spoke of a wife submitting to her husband, he was calling for a voluntary response on the wife's part to willingly cooperate with her husband and take on the responsibility of bearing his burden with him and for him. Paul reminded wives that this matter "is fitting in the Lord." In other words, this is how the Lord has designed the family to work.

Wives, God has called you to a voluntary cooperation with your husbands. The fact that the wife is to submit to the husband indicates that the husband has been given a role of headship. He is responsible before God for the family and its wellbeing. The wife is to willingly cooperate in this matter. She is not to fight against her husband but cooperate with him, thus bringing unity to the family.

Husbands

Paul knew some men would take this matter of being the head in the wrong way. Many men have believed that because they were the head of the home, they could demand anything of their wives and children. Paul reminded husbands that they were not to be harsh with their wives but to love them. Gentleness, compassion, and humility would keep these husbands from being harsh. They were to respect their wives and be considerate of them in love. They were to take an example from Christ and his love for them.

Christ loves us with tenderness and compassion. His love for us is such that he willingly laid down his life. This is how husbands need to love their wives. If you truly love your wife, you will lay down your life for her. This means that you will die to yourself, your comforts, and your interests when necessary to minister to her. A godly husband will literally die for his wife. She in turn is to willingly cooperate with him, as a helper and partner. It is quite easy to see how this kind of relationship would work, with each person unselfishly serving the other.

Children

Paul told the children to obey their parents in everything because this is what would please the Lord. We should not assume that this would always be easy. It would require a sacrificing of the child's interests and desires for the sake of the parent. Observing a respectful relationship between the parents would help a child behave unselfishly. The assumption here was that these families were Christian families. However, there would have also been unbelieving families in Colosse. These unbelieving parents might desire their child to do something contrary to the will and purpose of God. In such a case, the child would have to obey God rather than the parents (Acts 5:29). The assumption was that the Christian parent wanted only to glorify the Lord in all things and would not ask the child to do anything contrary to the will and purpose of God.

Fathers

Paul spoke next to fathers. He commanded them to be careful not to embitter their children. They were to be especially careful that they didn't frustrate their children, causing them to become discouraged. It is quite possible to place so many demands on a child that the spirit of the child is broken. This can result in the child becoming bitter and discouraged. Paul understood this problem and challenged the fathers in particular to be careful to take into consideration the nature of their children. They were to love them and nourish them, but they were not to crush them, lest the children give up hope. It is unclear why this would be particularly a problem for men. It might be that fathers are often tempted to push their children beyond their abilities to endure.

Slaves

A common aspect of Colossian society was slavery. Paul did not encourage this practice. He spoke about slavery here simply because it was already part of Colossian society. He believed that slaves were as important in the kingdom as free men and women.

Paul told the slaves to obey their earthly masters in everything. They were to obey whether or not the master was watching them. As slaves, they were to do their best and win the favor of their masters. They were to serve their masters with sincere hearts and reverence for the Lord God. Paul made a connection between the slave's service for the master and reverence for the Lord God.

This same principle applies in the work we do. We all have bosses or people to whom we are accountable in this life. We are to serve them with an honest and sincere heart. As we do this, we show reverence for the Lord who has put us in this position. In verse 23 Paul challenges us to do everything with all our heart, because we are actually working for the Lord. People might not see what we are doing, but God does and he will hold us accountable. He will reward us or judge us according to our actions and attitudes here below. That includes our attitudes toward our earthly bosses as well. We must see our service for an earthly authority as a way of serving our heavenly authority.

In verse 25 Paul reminded slaves that anyone who did wrong was to be punished for that wrong. There was to be no favoritism. It may have been that there were Christian slaves expecting that because their masters were Christian as well, then they should not be punished for doing wrong. They may have thought that they could take certain liberties with a Christian master because they were brothers in Christ. Paul told the slaves that this was not the case. There was to be no special treatment for Christian slaves. They were to be as justly punished as unbelieving slaves.

Masters

Paul then challenged masters to provide for their slaves (4:1). Masters were not to cheat slaves or mistreat them in any way but to be careful to provide them with all they needed. These Spirit-filled masters were to be generous to their slaves and treat them with respect. They were to do this, according to Paul, because they also had a Master in heaven. In other words, they were accountable to God, as their slaves were accountable to them. They would have to answer to God for how they treated their slaves.

What Paul is telling us here is that because we have been united with Christ in his death and resurrection, we have a special obligation toward God. Our relationship with the Lord Jesus means that we are obligated not only to honor God, but also to honor our fellow human beings.

For Consideration:

- What does it mean for a wife to submit to her husband? Does this mean that the husband can control her and tell her to do whatever he wants?

- How does true love keep the husband from controlling his wife?

- What example do we have in the Lord Jesus to help us to understand what it means to love?

- Take a moment to consider your work. Do you serve at work in such a way that God is pleased with you?

- What does Paul have to say here about breaking the spirit of a child? How can the spirit of a child be broken, leading to discouragement?

For Prayer:

- If you are a wife, ask the Lord to help you to willingly cooperate with your husband.

- If you are a husband, ask the Lord to help you to love your wife and willingly deny yourself for her needs.

- If you are a parent, ask the Lord to keep you from discouraging your children.

- Ask the Lord to help you to do your work as if you were working only for him.

20

Prayer, Wisdom, and Grace

Read Colossians 4:2–6

Much of this epistle to the Colossians is devoted to challenging believers to live the life that God requires of them. As I have been working through this study, I have personally been struggling with the tension between how Paul began this letter and how he ended it. Paul took much time in the beginning of his letter to show the Colossians that the law has no value when it comes to salvation. He made it very clear that when Jesus died on the cross, there was not another thing that needed to be done to accomplish salvation. Jesus took our sins and the law with him on that cross.

As Paul moved on to the second half of his epistle, he spent much time explaining to believers how they needed to live their new life in Christ. Paul challenged his readers to seek to be perfect in their character and behavior. He called them to deal honorably in all their relationships in the body of Christ. He went into some detail to show them that they had an obligation to God because of what the Lord Jesus had done for them. Paul challenged the Colossians to be careful how they represented the Lord in their community. The question I have been asking myself is this, "If we are not under law, why do we have so many obligations?" Before examining what Paul has to tell us in Chapter 4, I want to speak briefly to this issue.

We need to understand that when we place ourselves under the law, we are saying that what Jesus did is not sufficient. If we feel that we need to keep the law to get to heaven or to remain in God's good favor, we have failed to understand what the Lord Jesus did on the cross. What he did on the cross was enough to cover all my sin. I will fail on many occasions in this life, but Christ's death covers it all. I can rest assured that his death is enough. I do not need to add anything to his work. I can rest completely in what he has done. To think that I need to do more is to devalue the work of Christ on the cross. It is by Christ's work *only* that I am saved. The law has nothing to do with my salvation. Even those who lived under the Mosaic law were not saved by keeping it but through repentance and faith (Psalm 51:16–17; Habakkuk 2:4).

The second thing we need to understand here is that if we place ourselves under the law, we must live by the law and keep it completely. If you choose to try to get to heaven by means of the law, you have to realize that if you fail even once, you will not get there. Apart from Christ, there is not a single person who ever was able to keep the law perfectly. We are guilty of breaking the law of God in our thoughts and actions (Romans 3:23). Beyond this is the fact that we were born with a sin nature (Psalm 51:5; Ephesians 2:3). This in itself is enough to condemn us even before we have a chance to disobey.

We need to understand that it is not the heart of God that we focus on obeying a set of rules and regulations. His desire is that we focus on him and respond from our heart in love. We can do the right thing, but if it is not done in love, what does it really mean? (1 Corinthians 13:3) Too many people lift up that law as an idol and bow down to it, believing that in so doing they are worshiping and honoring God. But in reality they are guilty of idolatry. The central focus of the believer is not law but Christ. We live for him, not from obligation but from love. We do not pat ourselves on the back because we measured up to a set of standards. We recognize our guilt and understand that we could never be perfect, but we rejoice in Christ's perfection and what he has done for us. We delight from the heart to follow him and be like him.

I am saved from my sins through Christ whether I keep the law or not. This does not mean that I can live irresponsibly. It does not mean that I have no obligations to Christ. It does mean, however, that I will not put my trust in the law to bring me into a good relationship with the Father. I will trust alone in what Jesus has done. I follow the principles that God has laid out in his Word, not because they are law and will grant me special favor with God but because they are right and good.

Prayer

Having said this, it is important that we move on to speak about Paul's challenge to the Colossians in verses 2–7. In verse 2 Paul challenged the Colossians to devote themselves to prayer. The word *devote* indicates that that they were to be steadfast in prayer. To devote oneself to something is to give oneself continually to the object of devotion. This is what Paul was challenging the Colossians to do. One of the things we need to understand is that we are in constant need of the Lord, his wisdom and his direction. Through prayer we seek him and that direction. Paul was reminding the Colossians that they needed to be a people led of the Spirit. This meant that they needed to commit their ways to him in all that they did. They were to seek him, his counsel and guidance through prayer, and then listen to him for that direction. Paul told them that this was to be a constant practice. In other words, they were to earnestly seek the Lord in everything. Prayer for believers ought to be as natural as breathing.

Notice in verse 2 that Paul told the Colossians that as they devoted themselves to prayer, they needed to be watchful and thankful. Watchfulness could have several aspects. Those who are watchful in their prayers expect an answer. They pray and then wait in confident expectation to see how the Lord God will answer. Do we have this type of faith? How often have we prayed without any sense that God was going to answer our prayer? Those who pray in faith watch earnestly for the answer.

Another aspect of watchfulness involves seeking guidance on the content of prayers. There are many needs all around us in this world. How many people does God bring to us in the course of the day? He brings these people to us so that we can minister to them. He brings them to us so we can lift them up in prayer. If we watch carefully, God will show us specifically what he wants us to be praying for in the course of the day. Watch to see the needs that he brings before you. Pray about those needs in particular and in faith commit them to him.

Paul also told the Colossians to be thankful as they prayed. Believers can only be thankful when they recognize that God is in control of all that happens. If we are going to be thankful, we need to surrender to God and what he is doing in our life. How many times have we complained and grumbled to God about the things that were happening to us? Paul is telling us that we need to be thankful in prayer. We need to surrender to God and accept his purpose. We need to cast off our grumbling and complaining and learn to thank God that he is in control and that he loves us. To pray with thankfulness is to pray with confidence in God's plan. It is to pray with trust in his purpose. It is to surrender to him and his will. We may not understand what God is doing, but we come with faith and confidence that he knows what is best. We pray with a thankful heart.

In verse 3 Paul asked the Colossians to pray for him as well. He asked them to pray particularly that a door would be opened for him to preach the gospel. Notice that he was in chains at the time of this writing. His chains did not discourage him, however. Even in his chains, Paul asked God to use him and to give him opportunities to share the Word with clarity. How easy it would be for Paul to feel that he could no longer preach the gospel in his chains! The fact of the matter is that no matter where we are and no matter what circumstance we find ourselves in, we can share the truth of God. It may not be easy. It may not be in the way we have been accustomed to sharing, but wherever we are the Lord calls us to open our eyes to the opportunities before us. This was the cry of Paul. He asked the Colossians to pray for him so that he would see the opportunities that abounded around him to share the love of the Lord Jesus.

Wisdom

Paul told the Colossians that they were also to be wise in the way they acted toward the unbeliever, who was outside the salvation of the Lord Jesus. Paul encouraged the Colossians to be very careful in how they lived their lives before the watching world. As Christians, they represented the Lord Jesus in all they did. Whether it was in their business dealings or in their families, they were sharing Christ by means of their example. People need to see the reality of the power of God demonstrated in our lives through ordinary activity. They need to see that what we are saying is real. We can show this by the way we live before them. We are to be very careful to demonstrate in real life the truth of what we preach.

Notice that Paul told the Colossians in verse 5 that they were to make the most of every opportunity. In other words, they needed to seek out opportunities to demonstrate to the world the reality of what the Lord Jesus had done on the cross. If our neighbors are in need, we are to reach out to them. If they are hungry, we are to feed them. There are many ways we can demonstrate the love of the Lord. We are to do our best to take advantage of these opportunities. It is important that we preach the gospel, but it is just as important that we live out the reality of the gospel before all whom God brings before us. Wisdom is the practical application of truth to real life. We are called to be a wise people.

Grace

In verse 6 Paul told the Colossians that they were to let their conversation be full of grace. The Greek word for *conversation* here is the word *logos,* which literally means "word." The idea is that whatever words we speak are to be full of grace. When our words are full of grace, they are words that bring blessing. They are thankful, honest, and kind. These words build up and do not tear down. They demonstrate a gracious and positive attitude. When we are with someone whose words are gracious, we are lifted up. We are encouraged and blessed. Have you ever been with someone who is negative? This is a weakness I must admit that I have. I have often had to go to the Lord to ask for help in seeing things from a more positive perspective. I don't think I am alone in this problem. God wants our words to build up and bless others.

Notice that Paul told the Colossians that their words needed to be seasoned with salt. There are several things about salt we need to understand. Salt purifies and preserves. Salt enhances the flavor of food and brings out the best in that food. This is what Paul was saying. When we answer people, especially those who upset us, we are to season our words with purifying salt. We are to allow the salt of the Holy Spirit to bring from our spirit the very best. We are to allow the salt of the Spirit to purify and cleanse our words so that they bring honor to the Lord Jesus.

Paul is telling us here that we need to be a people who properly represent the Lord Jesus in all we do. We are to seek him earnestly and continually in prayer. We are not only to share the Lord Jesus in word but also in deed. Paul challenges us to seek opportunities to share the Lord Jesus by demonstrating his love in practical ways. We are to be positive and gracious in how we speak. How we live and speak reflects what we truly believe.

For Consideration:

• What does Paul teach us about thankfulness in prayer?

• How does God want you to use your current circumstances to share his love?

• What do we learn here about sharing God's love by our actions?

• Why is it important that we learn to speak with grace? How does this impact our witness for the Lord Jesus?

For Prayer:

• Ask the Lord to teach you how to devote yourselves more fully to prayer.

• Ask the Lord to show you the opportunities he is bringing to you each day to share his love in a practical way.

- Ask the Lord to help you to be positive and gracious in your words so that you build up the body and demonstrate by how you speak that he is in control.

21

Final Greetings

Read Colossians 4:7–18

I n this final section of Chapter 4, Paul sent greetings from a variety of individuals to the church in Colosse. We will examine each of these individuals separately.

The first person Paul mentioned was a man by the name of Tychicus. Paul was sending Tychicus to the church in Colosse for him to tell them how Paul was doing. Paul considered Tychicus to be a dear brother. He had also proven to be a faithful worker for the gospel. Paul wanted Tychicus to encourage the church in Colosse with news of his circumstances. Obviously, the church would be very concerned about Paul, knowing that he was in prison. It is quite interesting to see here that in the midst of Paul's imprisonment, his concern was not for himself but for those who might be grieving for him. Paul sent Tychicus to encourage the church regarding their concerns.

Tychicus was not going alone to Colosse. He was taking with him a man by the name of Onesimus. We read about

Onesimus in the book of Philemon. He was a slave who had robbed his master, Philemon. After he escaped, he came to know the Lord and proved to be very useful to Paul in his imprisonment. Paul sent him back to his master in Colosse. Paul considered Onesimus to be a very dear brother in Christ. Onesimus had wronged his master, but he had come to know the Lord and was willing to make things right. Paul looked past what Onesimus had done to his present usefulness.

Although Paul was sending Tychicus and Onesimus, other brothers were not able to visit the church in Colosse. Paul spoke in verse 10 of a fellow prisoner by the name of Aristarchus. From Acts 19:29 and Acts 27:2 we understand that Aristarchus was from the city of Thessalonica and was a traveling companion of the apostle Paul.

Paul sent greetings from Mark, the cousin of Barnabas. Mark had been a fellow traveler with Paul but had abandoned him during a missionary journey. Barnabas chose to take Mark on a subsequent missionary trip, but Paul so strongly disagreed with this decision that Paul and Barnabas separated and went their own ways. What is significant here is that Paul seems to have resolved the differences that existed between him and Mark. Paul encouraged the church in Colosse to receive Mark warmly.

In verse 11 Paul wrote of a man by the name of Jesus who was also called Justus. He was a Jew who had come to know the Lord Jesus. He, along with the others mentioned here, had proven to be a real comfort to Paul in his time of need. God used fellow believers to minister to Paul in his time of imprisonment.

Greetings also came from Epaphras, who was from the region of Colosse. He had left Colosse to minister to Paul in prison (see Colossians 1:7). He sent his greetings to the church in Colosse. Epaphras in particular wrestled in prayer for the Colossians. His cry to God was for this church to remain firm in the will of God. His desire was that they be mature and fully assured in their faith. Paul told the Colossians that Epaphras was working very hard for them in ministering to Paul and his needs.

Paul's old traveling companion Luke, who was a doctor, also sent his greetings to the church in Colosse. Demas too greeted the church. From 2 Timothy 4:10 we understand that Demas would eventually abandon Paul. He would do this because of his love for the world.

Paul personally sent his greetings to the church of Laodicea as well as to a woman by the name of Nympha, who had a church in her house. Paul encouraged the church in Colosse to pass this letter on to the church in Laodicea so that they could read it. He also told them that he had written a letter to the church in Laodicea that they should read. While this letter to the Laodicean church is not contained in the Scriptures, it was still written by Paul. Not all that Paul wrote is found in the Scriptures, but what we have is what God saw fit to give us for our instruction in all righteousness (2 Timothy 3:16–17).

In verse 17 Paul told the church in Colosse to tell Archippus to complete the work he had received from the Lord. We read about Archippus in verse 2 of Philemon. We are not told what work this man had undertaken. Could it be that he was discouraged in his ministry? What Paul told him here would have been a challenge to him to continue.

In conclusion, Paul wrote a greeting to the Colossians in his own hand. A secretary wrote many of his letters, but on occasion to make a letter more personal, Paul would write some words himself. He concluded by asking the Colossians to remember his chains. In other words, they were to keep him before God in prayer. They were to pray for him in his imprisonment.

In all this we see how personal Paul was. He knew individuals by name, not only in Colosse but also in all the other areas where he worked. For Paul, the ministry in

which he was involved was about people. It was not about
how many churches he started but about real people and real
needs.

For Consideration:

- What does this section tell us about Paul's concern for
  individuals?

- Could it be said that Paul had more concern for others
  than for his own needs? Explain.

- What evidence is there in this chapter that shows that
  Paul was able to overlook past faults and move on in his
  relationships with people? Where do you stand on this?

For Prayer:

- Ask the Lord to give you a greater concern for
  individuals.

- Ask the Lord to set you free from thinking only of your
  needs and your problems. Ask him to open your eyes to
  the needs of others around you.

- Ask the Lord to forgive you for the times when ministry
  has become more about numbers and programs than
  about people.

Light To My Path
Devotional Commentary Series

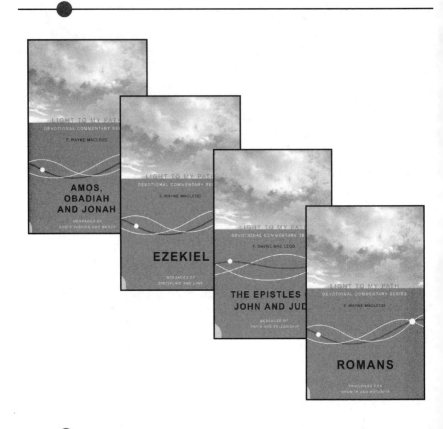

Now Available

Old Testament

- Ezra, Nehemiah, and Esther
- Ezekiel
- Amos, Obadiah, and Jonah
- Micah, Nahum, Habakkuk, and Zephaniah

New Testament

- John
- Acts
- Romans
- The Epistles of John and Jude

A new commentary series
for every day devotional use.

———————————————————————————●———————

"I am impressed by what I have read from this set of commentaries. I have found them to be concise, insightful, inspiring, practical and, above all, true to Scripture. Many will find them to be excellent resources."

Randy Alcorn

director of Eternal Perspective Ministries,
Author of *The Grace & Truth Paradox*
and *Money, Possessions & Eternity*

———————————————————————————●———————

New in the series
Spring 2005

Old Testament

• Isaiah
• Haggai, Zechariah and Malachi

New Testament

• Philippians and Colossians
• James and 1 & 2 Peter

Other books available from Authentic Media . . .

Authentic
MEDIA

129 Mobilization Drive
Waynesboro, GA 30830

706-554-1594
1-8MORE-BOOKS
ordersusa@stl.org
www.authenticbooks.com

An Introduction To The New Testament
Three Volume Collection

D. Edmond Hiebert

Though not a commentary, the Introduction to the New Testament presents each book's message along with a discussion of such questions as authorship, composition, historical circumstances of their writing, issues of criticism and provides helpful, general information on their content and nature. The bibliographies and annotated book list are extremely helpful for pastors, teachers, and laymen as an excellent invitation to further careful exploration.

This book will be prized by all who have a desire to delve deeply into the New Testament writings.

Volume 1: The Gospels And Acts
Volume 2: The Pauline Epistles
Volume 3: The Non-Pauline Epistles and Revelation

1-884543-74-X   976 Pages

Cat and Dog Theology
Rethinking Our Relationship With Our Master

Bob Sjogren & Dr. Gerald Robison

There is a joke about cats and dogs that conveys their differences perfectly.

> A dog says, "You pet me, you feed me, you shelter me, you love me, you must be God."
>
> A cat says, "You pet me, you feed me, you shelter me, you love me, I must be God."

These God-given traits of cats ("You exist to serve me") and dogs ("I exist to serve you") are often similar to the theological attitudes we have in our view of God and our relationship to Him. Using the differences between cats and dogs in a light-handed manner, the authors compel us to challenge our thinking in deep and profound ways. As you are drawn toward God and the desire to reflect His glory in your life, you will worship, view missions, and pray in a whole new way. This life-changing book will give you a new perspective and vision for God as you delight in the God who delights in you.

1-884543-17-0   224 Pages